SATURDAY NIGHT FEVER PITCH

THE MAGIC AND MADNESS OF FOOTBALL STYLE

SIMON DOONAN

LAURENCE KING PUBLISHING

For the fans

CONTENTS

Pride and Glory, or pain and suffering? The lavish oversized script chosen by Man Utd defender and Argentine international Marcos Rojo must have hurt like hell.

Boots, Balls and Balenciaga

I love nothing more than to contemplate Andy Carroll's man bun. I am fascinated by the bravado of Marcos Rojo's 'Pride' and 'Glory' leg tattoos. I never fail to marvel at the transformative power of Jamie Vardy's skinny suits (he cleans up well). Where others see reasons for mockery – a swishy sarong, a bleached mohawk, a camo-painted Bentley – I see mysterious self-disclosure, creativity, swagger and style. The unapologetic flamboyance of the star players is now an established part of football culture. This is the lens through which I view the world of footie. I am, therefore, less 'Fever Pitch' and more 'Saturday Night Fever Pitch'.

Up the Biscuits!

My footie journey began in my hometown of Reading in the late 1950s. Today Reading FC players are nicknamed the Royals. Back then they were dubbed the Biscuitmen, a homage to the Huntley & Palmers factory that belched fumes on the horizon. You could see it clearly from the window of our lav. Extracting enjoyment from the rain-lashed terraces of Elm Park was challenging, with my view of any dynamic plays being frequently blocked by a wall of threadbare demob suits and filthy John Collier overcoats. The word c*nt filled the air. Gradually I began to lose interest.

When I was 11, fate intervened. Something fabulous happened, something utterly brilliant which assured the future of my footie passions forever: I failed the 11-plus exam. If this had not happened, I would probably never have gone to another football game. At the Reading grammar schools it was all about rugby and cricket, but at my 11-plus-failure school, it was footie, footie, footie.

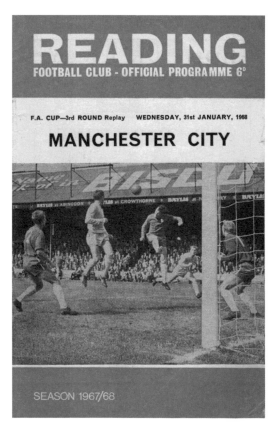

Of all the Reading games I attended in my teenage years, one in particular remains lodged in the memory. On 27 January 1968 the Biscuitmen – Dennis Allen, Colin Meldrum, Dave Bacuzzi, Ron Bayliss, Ernie Yard, Roger Smee and the rest of the lads – headed to Manchester City for the first game of the FA Cup Third Round Proper. A stunned crowd of 40,000 watched as our Biscuits held their own for a 0:0 draw. Quel shock! A replay at Elm Park was immediately scheduled.

The build-up to the 31 January rematch was mega. On the horizon, the biscuit factory began belching fumes of solidarity. Finally we would get to see some major stars including Glyn Pardoe, Neil Young, Colin 'Nijinsky' Bell and ... drumroll ... the great Mike 'Buzzer' Summerbee. Though awed at the prospect of the visiting luminaries, we were nonetheless confident of victory.

I can still remember that horrible sinking feeling as the Man City lads scored goal after goal. The final tally was 7:0. (I recently had the opportunity to exhume this buried trauma. On 8 April 2017, I schlepped all the way to Norwich to see my old home team take on the Canaries. Reading lost 7:1.) During the dying minutes of the game, I vividly recall my schoolmates doing something they had never done before: hurling vile personal insults at the opposing team. I remember a pal named Stuart ranting vengefully at Summerbee – he scored three of the seven goals – about his legendary conk.

Summerbee had something which – no offence to the Biscuitmen of yore – I had only observed on our telly. He had glamour, charisma, celebrity and style. And I liked his big nose. But most importantly he was best mates with (and here we come to the real elephant in the room, the entire *raison d'être* of my *raison d'être*, and the catalyst for the book that you are holding in your hot little hands) the greatest, handsomest, most spiffily attired and most legendary footballing folk-hero of all time: Georgie Best.

George Best – the Fifth Beatle, the bloke with the Jag and the swag – is, was and always will be the ground zero, the patron saint, of footballer fashion. The year before the Man City debacle, amid a flurry of publicity, 'Buzzer' Summerbee and George Best had merged their talents in a manner which had blown my style-crazed mind. They had opened a boutique, *together!* These two extraordinary players, exceptional athletes from deadly opposing Manchester teams … *they liked fashion too!*

'They sang songs about my nose, so I'd go and blow it on the corner flag to antagonize them. You could do that then; football was different in those days.'

Mike Summerbee, interviewed by Tom Bryant in *The Guardian*

> '**The Best entourage is glamorous and noisy.
> Jewellery glitters, silk collides with fur, faces are
> constantly recognized as belonging to the famous.**'
>
> Arthur Hopcraft on George Best

For me there was something magnificently life-affirming about George Best's vanity and his uncomplicated enjoyment of dressing up. He was our working-class lad made good, a stylish, gap-toothed Adonis. Back then glamorous George, and the legions of footie players who followed his lead, offered a beacon of hope to me, and to anyone attempting to escape a grim biscuit factory backstory.

With George as their pied piper, a new generation of players discovered the delights of swag, diving into a world of sharkskin suits, polo necks, medallions, Cuban heels, Chelsea boots, hip-hugger pants and E-Types. Simply put, *they went stark raving mod*.

And so it is with the football stars of today, only more so. With their Ferraris, their mental haircuts, their Louis Vuitton monogrammed wheelies, their tattoos and their Givenchy growling Rottweiler T-shirts, contemporary cash-rich footie players transcend their working-class origins with that same playful mix of flash and optimism. You may be from the wrong side of the tracks, but if you work hard and get lucky, you too can reinvent yourself and evade your biscuit factory destiny. Or, at least, attempt to. Yes, at times today's lads, with their obscene mega-wealth, appear a tad nouveau riche, but better to be nouveau riche than nouveau poor. Right?

George Best of Man Utd and Man City's Mike Summerbee, improbable fashion mavericks, c. 1967.

11

It's just 'andbags.
**Mario Balotelli toting his
toiletries in an $825 Damier-
print Louis Vuitton clutch.**

> '**I** could never have worn the silly skin-tight shirts they wear now, my gut **was that bad**.'

Paul Merson, recalling his Arsenal heyday

1. Dedicated Footballers of Fashion

The Style Tribes of Soccer

Today's football players are the most fashionable, style-obsessed sportsmen in history. Possessed of a natural elegance, these wiry young studs – Ramos, Giroud, Piqué, Sánchez, Ramsey, Sturridge, Sterling, Bale, Agüero, Walcott et al. – are the perfect canvas for today's retro biker leathers and nut-mangling jeans.

Not only do the lads have the requisite build, but they also dig it, big time. Whether from Nigeria, Bahia or Essex, today's footie stars are unapologetically fashion-addicted. And, God bless 'em, they pay full retail. Why? Because they can!

Juan Mata's 2014 transfer fee from Chelsea to Manchester United was a jockstrap-shrivelling £40 million. Allegedly he now earns about £150,000 per week. Other players are making even vaster sums of money. Argentinian Carlos Tevez recently signed on to play for Shanghai Shenhua for £650,000 a week, more than twice the salary of Cristiano Ronaldo. But Mata did something these other high earners have yet to do: in 2016 he acknowledged how batshit crazy it all was: 'It's like we live in a bubble. Compared to the rest of society, we earn a ridiculous amount. It's unfathomable.'

'There's a word you don't hear around footballers' dressing rooms any more – mortgage.'

Niall Quinn, former Sunderland striker, 2002

Clubs spend recklessly on players, and players in turn spend recklessly on … *everything!* These overpaid peacocks feed the economy. They buy shit – Birkins for the wife, a mock Tudor for mum and dad, marathon online-gambling sessions, fancy wines and a Ferrari or two. But then what? Then everything: £5000 Tom Ford tuxes, £700 Givenchy T-shirts, £3500 Saint Laurent biker jackets, £600 Dolce & Gabbana jeans, £650 Margiela trainers, £900 Moncler puffer coats, £23,000 diamond-encrusted Rolex watches, and mountains of other stuff from cheaper joints like Zara and Topman.

The cash-rich footie/fashion landscape has never been more entertainingly chaotic than it is today. Is there anything, you are tempted to ask, that these pampered popinjays will not throw on their bodies? Closer examination reveals that distinct categories are in play. Today's fashionable footballers fall into five principal teams: the Good Taste Ambassadors, the Label Kings, the Psychedelic Ninjas, the Hired Assassins and, finally, the Bohemians and Fauxhemians. Allow me to guide you through the magic and madness of these fashion squads.

The Good Taste Ambassadors

'Footballers are only interested in drinking, clothes, and the size of their willies', claimed Birmingham City managing director Karren Brady in 1994. Not true! Not every successful footie player drives around drunk in a mink-lined glow-in-the-dark Lamborghini, wearing a skin-tight D-Squared jumpsuit while jangling Chrome Hearts man-jewellery from every limb and obsessing about the size of his tackle. There is a large and significant group of players who are actively rebelling against all the clichéd notions of flashy dressing and conspicuous consumption. For every Elvis there is a Duke of Windsor. For every unhinged spendaholic there is a Good Taste Ambassador.

Arsenal's all-time record goalscorer, Thierry Henry, oozing good taste.

Like many of the painfully earnest good-tasters, Steven George Gerrard MBE – the former Liverpool legend is currently serving as an academy coach for his old team – is no longer in the first flush of youth. Along with Andrea Pirlo he has entered his wine-instead-of-lager, dilfy years. Graziano Pellè – at the time of writing one of the top ten highest-paid players in the world, having shot off to China to play for Shandong Luneng – is headed in the same Ambassadorial direction. Would you expect anything less from a lad who almost became a professional ballroom dancer? Ambassadors retire, but fortunately there is no shortage of tasteful replacements waiting in the wings to grab the Ambassadorial sash: Alvaro Morata, Chelsea's new golden boy, dresses with the classy restraint of a Spanish aristo.

The *ne plus ultra* of Good Taste Ambassadors is surely former Bayern Munich central midfielder Xabi Alonso. Like many members of this conventional tribe, Xabi is vocal about his aversion to bling, stating, 'I don't wear earrings and necklaces. The only piece of jewellery I wear is a watch.' According to Spanish newspaper *MARCA*, Signor Alonso is so elegant, 'he could even play in a suit and tie'. Online fashion journal Mr Porter also used the 'e' word, describing him as 'understated, commanding and elegant'. If anyone ever described me that way I would drink antifreeze – and not before

'I do like fashion.
I like to look pristine,
clean and classy.'

Steven Gerrard to MrPorter.com, 2016

bludgeoning the complimenter to death – but for a Good Taste Ambassador like Xabi, or the now-retired Thierry Henry, this kind of heartfelt commentary is music to his well-tweezed, elegant ears.

There are three basic reasons why a particular footie player might retreat from the I-just-won-the-pools world of high-priced designer flash and elect to become a Good Taste Ambassador. First, image rehab. Wearing conventional smart clothes – as opposed to MC Hammer pants and a Buffalo hat – can help to expunge transgressions and improve your public perception. Second, the player in question has exhausted his tolerance for being mocked on social media for his avant-garde fashion choices. But the final and most popular reason is that the player is reaching the end of his career and is desperate to be perceived as a bloke who is now ready for future big-boy opportunities – as a manager, a pundit or a full-blown brand. Nobody is going to hire you to shill their cars/watches/health-food drinks if you ponce about all Gangnam style, goes the line of thinking.

The Label Kings

Spring 2016. The house of Saint Laurent elects to memorialize the 1969 Moon landing by designing a tapestry funnel-neck blouson. Who on Earth would plonk down $2690 to own this garment? A footballer, of course – Netherlands forward Memphis Depay. Conclusion: Mr Depay is a Label King.

I do not regard the phrase 'Label King' as an insult. *Au contraire*, Label Kings are a force for good. While pampered red-carpet celebs whine for freebies and discounts on designer clothing, Label King footie players are happy to splurge. They feed the fashion economy. Long live the Label Kings, regardless of which label they wear.

Among the Label Kings sub-tribes proliferate, as certain designer brands seem to hold particular appeal. Chief among the sub-tribes, at least in numbers, are the Vuitton Victors. When players arrive at or leave the stadium they are expected to display an air of focused militaristic neatness. Wear your blazer. No goofy hats or gangsta shades. But fashion will out. Footballers being footballers, they will always find a way to fly their fashion flag. Enter the player's old friend, Louis Vuitton.

The house of Louis Vuitton – the most counterfeited brand in the world and the company that makes the carrying case for the FIFA World Cup trophy – has a history which parallels that of football. Founded by Louis Vuitton in 1854, the company pre-dates the founding of the first football club (Sheffield United in 1857) by only three years. In 1896 Louis's son Georges rolled out the iconic LV monogram canvas print. A century later the cash-rich, prestige-acquiring footballers of the world are mainlining all things Vuitton, a blinding cavalcade of washbags, wheelies and backpacks.

One small step for Memphis.
#saintlaurent

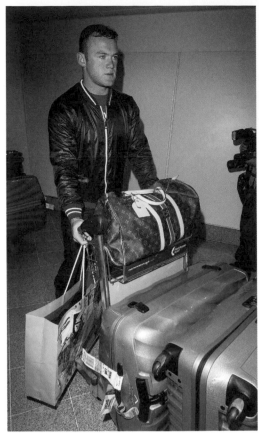

Above left When you are the captain of both Real Madrid and the Spanish national team you can mash up your logos and hang the consequences: Sergio Ramos daringly teams his Louis Vuitton wheelie with a Gucci washbag.

Above right Wayne Rooney pushes wife Coleen's Louis Vuitton. Sigmund Freud, who claimed that handbags were 'vaginal symbols', would have had a field day with this picture.

Hot on the Vuitton Victors' monogrammed heels are the Gucci Gladiators. Drenched in glamour and controversy since the opening of the first Gucci store in Florence in 1920, the Gucci brand has always flaunted that logo with unabashed pride. Just like many of the best footballers, Gucci advertising images have often walked the line between acceptable and offensive. In 2003 a Gucci 'spread' shot by Mario Testino depicted a headless Carmen Kass, pants down, flaunting a pubic topiary in the shape of a G.

Gucci's unique combo of history, craftsmanship and contemporary erotic sizzle has made this brand a favourite with players the world over. Label King footballers and their WAGs are frequently to be seen cramming ramparts of Gucci shopping bags into the minuscule boots of their supercars.

In short, Label Kings are a tribe of status-conscious footie players who are mesmerized by designer logos. Cristiano Ronaldo snoozes on his private plane under Hermès H blankets. Liverpool striker Daniel Sturridge keeps his eye creams in a $1000 Goyard designer washbag. Even Leicester City striker Jamie Vardy crams his personal effects into an MCM studded and monogrammed backpack.

Above left West Ham right back Pablo Zabaleta teams his Gucci monogrammed blouson with the footie player's preferred style of jean: the distressed skinny.

Above right Real Madrid forward, and unrepentant Label King, Cristiano Ronaldo is a longtime Gucci devotee, frequently sporting the logo – as per the infamous Gucci ad – in the pubic region.

Right He helped propel Leicester City to the historic 2015/16 Premier League win, so there's no reason why Jamie Vardy should not treat himself to a designer accessory – very useful for schlepping his kit, not to mention a bag or two of his 'Vardy Salted' Walkers crisps.

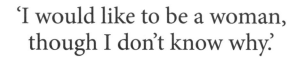

'I would like to be a woman, though I don't know why.'

Djibril Cissé, France striker, on owning a
Jean Paul Gaultier dress, 2003

Left 'I buy a lot of interesting clothes and I have
never bought an item, got it home and thought,
"I can't wear that, it's ridiculous"', Djibril Cissé
(pictured in Givenchy kilt and sweatshirt) told
FourFourTwo magazine in 2017.

Above Man Utd midfielder Paul Pogba is taking the
Cissé legacy – road-warrior + peroxide + studs +
ink + not remotely caring what other people think
– and running with it. Note the T-shirt: at the time
of writing there is a mania among Label Kings and
Psychedelic Ninjas for all things Givenchy. The logo
may be hidden, but there is no mistaking those
rabid Rottweilers.

The Psychedelic Ninjas

The Psychedelic Ninjas are, as the name might suggest, the most provocative and polarizing component of today's footie/fashion firmament. Psychedelic Ninjas, in their studded Philipp Plein leather jackets, jaunty chapeaux and Comme des Garçons man-blouses, are avant-garde extremists who push the boundaries of convention. Among Psychedelic Ninjas, styles vary from punk to full-blown clown. The one thing they all have in common is a commendable disregard for the opinions of others.

Djibril Cissé, the tattooed road-warrior with the blond mohawk and Mr Magoo eyewear is, in many ways, the grand-daddy of the Psychedelic Ninjas. During his high-profile career – he recently retired due to leg injuries – he took his exuberant Psychedelic Ninjadom and extrapolated it into all aspects of his life. While playing for Liverpool he bought a local pile and reinvented himself as the Lord of Frodsham Manor.

Formerly of Barcelona and now playing for PSG, Dani Alves is, in European competitions, the second most decorated foot-baller of all time (Maldini was top). You name it – the World Cup, the UEFA Champions League – and Ninja Dani has won it. When you are as mind-blowingly accomplished as he undoubtedly is, you have carte blanche to let your freak flag fly. And he does. Alves's taboo-busting approach to fashion is the gift that keeps on giving. No amount of social media blowback inhibits his fearless style choices.

Neymar, another Brazilian Psychedelic Ninja, might best be described as Bieber-goes-Manga. There is something jagged and undeniably cartoony about his finger-in-the-socket hair, pointy catlike features and super-skinny sharp-angled physique, invariably draped in outré Bieber-esque styles.

'I like many things. Bananas are good, of course, as are vases and chicken bones. But, I must say, I find it hard to look beyond old vials filled with various blood types.'

Dani Alves riffing on Fashion

Left Portuguese international Raul Meireles and his wife Ivone, flying the flag for the Psychedelic Ninjas and reminding us that dressing down is a crime against humanity.

Above Charles N'Zogbia is the former Aston Villa midfielder who made Psychedelic Ninja history when he showed up for practice in a floral two-piece, prompting many pundits to speculate that he had 'made it from his nan's couch'.

During the 2017 summer transfer window, Neymar exploded onto the back pages with the announcement that he was moving from Barcelona to Paris Saint-Germain, where he joins fellow Ninja Dani Alves. The price tag? £200 million, the most expensive transfer in footie history. Pundits and podcasters spent hours frantically parsing the Neymar deal in search of sinister motives. Not me. For Ninjas like Neymar and Alves, the motivation for the move to gay Paree is clear: better shopping.

Cameroonian Alex Song is yet another former Barça Ninja (one starts to wonder what the hell is going on in that dressing room at Camp Nou). His outlandish personal style makes Pharrell Williams look like a '50s bank clerk. 'Everyone who knows me really well knows that I love clothes and to dress well', Song once told the *Daily Mail*, revealing something deeply fascinating about the Psychedelic Ninjas: *they think they look perfectly normal!*

In conclusion, Psychedelic Ninjas are unconventional style provocateurs, life-enhancing individuals who make the world of footie a more interesting place. Dressing insanely is a fundamental human right. Looking like a maniac is hearty and healthy. Long live the Psychedelic Ninjas.

The Hired Assassins

Balotelli does it, as do Daley Blind and Samir Nasri. Didier Drogba rocks a croc version. Even retirees like David Beckham and Eric Cantona do it. Welcome to the super-butch world of the Hired Assassin. The Hired Assassin look is lean, mean, scrappy, edgy, and screams 'rough trade'. Wall-to-wall tattoos, sanded denims, worn leather – it's dressing like you're Jason Statham in a *Crank* movie.

Adopting the *sauvage* and sinister Hired Assassin look is thrilling and enervating. There is a whiff of sadism in those filthy Rag & Bone jeans, John Varvatos cargo pants and Diesel hoodies. It's a combo of high voltage and high function. The Hired Assassin

Left Just because you are a Spanish Chelsea central midfielder does not mean you cannot dress like a Russian hitman. Cesc Fàbregas looking tough and malevolent.

Above Chelsea left back Marcos Alonso looking sinister and invincible. The black eye is the perfect accessory.

US Navy aviators are the Assassin's signature adornment, seen here on Mario Balotelli.

underpins his look with normcore James Perse T-shirts. If it's chilly, then V-necked sweaters will be worn – à la Simon Cowell, but minus the moobs – over rock-hard chests. Navy and black are the Assassin colours. Trainers? Black or white. Jacket? There is a range of options: Schweinsteiger wears a zipped bomber. Samir Nasri rocks a designer biker jacket.

Why are today's players, blokes who could presumably afford to buy the most outré designer fashion, opting for the somewhat grim and understated Hired Assassin look in such overwhelming numbers? First, it reeks of testosterone. Hired Assassins are mega chick-magnets. Second, it's a low-maintenance, easy-breezy, non-iron look. And last, and most importantly: footie players – everyone from Joe Hart to Wayne Rooney – gravitate towards the Hired Assassin look because it is unimpeachable and hater-immune. Psychedelic Ninjas are an easy target for social media, but *nobody fucks with a Hired Assassin.*

Bohemians and Fauxhemians

In the past footballers had zero access to cool culture or groovy music. On the bus they were forced to listen to Tony Bennett, or whatever selection the boss dictated via the speaker system. Yes, they rubbed shoulders with celebs, but they were more likely to find themselves hanging out with Twinkle, Tony Blackburn or the Grumbleweeds than with Iggy Pop or the New York Dolls. Footballers have a long history of listening to – and adoring – un-hip music. Phil Neville loves Céline Dion. Steven Gerrard once clocked a DJ, allegedly, for refusing to play Phil Collins. I have an old '70s footie annual in which Jackie Charlton proudly lists whistling Roger Whittaker as his favourite recording artist.

Innovative music was anathema to footie, as were hippy-dippy clothes. 'What the fuck have I done?', asked England manager Alf Ramsey, when in 1972 long-haired Leicester striker Frank Worthington showed up at the airport attired in a head-to-toe Dennis Hopper outfit. Along with everyone else in Footie Universe, Sir Alf had a strong aversion to hippies and fops. They were seen as the kinds of bloke who might infect the team with nasty habits and 'alternative' ideas.

In recent years there has been a shift: not exactly a full-length embroidered burlap Mamas & the Papas muumuu, but a shift nonetheless. The reason for this change is simple – contemporary culture has become so vast and chaotic that nobody can quite keep track of what it means to be 'alternative' any more. Do Tim Howard's bald head and beard make him edgy? Are Sanskrit tattoos the sign of an Essex chav or a Brooklyn boho? Are hard-core Firm members allowed to drink organic brews?

For many years Footie World recoiled from counter-culture notions and bohemian fads. And then, in 2011, hardman West Ham striker Andy Carroll broke ranks, threw on the wellies and skipped off to Glastonbury.

'I'm obsessive about trainers. I've got about 300 pairs. I'm a real sneaker-head. I don't buy designer ones. Mine are old school. I've got them upstairs in my garage … I'm on eBay all the time.'

Ben Foster, West Bromwich Albion and England goalkeeper, 2013

Hidetoshi Nakata, the greatest Japanese footballer of all time, qualifies as hipster simply because he's Japanese. Like his fellow countrymen he can wear avant-garde styles and oversized eyewear without looking like he's trying too hard.

Everton's Leighton Baines (left) is a neo-mod hipster, as exemplified by the fact that he hangs out with Miles Kane, the co-frontman of hipster band The Last Shadow Puppets. According to Baines, 'Fashion ties in with music and football and we're both quite particular about how clothes sit on us, and we share the same tailor'.

Certain clubs, it should be noted, have developed a hipster reputation, though not many. Writing in *The Guardian* in 2015, Barry Glendenning makes a compelling case for the existence – in the entire universe – of six hipster clubs, including Dulwich Hamlet FC and Stonewall FC, Britain's first openly gay men's football team. Each listing comes with a caveat or two. For example, Barry applauds Germany's FC St. Pauli for its social justice position, but also points out that the club 'sells branded snow shovels in its ludicrously over-priced souvenir shop for an eye-watering €37'.

Change is coming slowly. Beards are proliferating and, hopefully, Leighton Baines is sharing his playlist. In the meantime those seeking more footie hipsters should probably focus on North America's MLS (Major League Soccer). Oblivious to the Euro-footie culture of Ferraris and oversized watches, US soccer players enjoy a much looser relationship with hipsterism. The epicentre of grungy Stateside bohemia resides with the Portland Timbers, whose woodsy crest is adorned with a heart-warming giant axe. The crunchy, bearded hipness of the Timbers knows no bounds: a tree is planted for every goal scored and stadium refreshments include barbecued-tofu sandwiches, spinach salads and chocolate-covered bacon. *Where are the bloody pies?*

Come fly with me! Style King George Best never had to ask twice. But what's with those ditsy curtains?

> 'I spent a lot of money on **booze, birds** and **fast cars**. The rest I just squandered.'
>
> George Best

2. Football's Kings of Style

The Fashion Hall of Fame

Once upon a time, player salaries were capped at a dismal £12 a week. Then, in 1961, Jimmy 'the Chin' Hill, all-around football luminary and president of the Professional Footballers' Association, success-fully lobbied for the abolition of the Football League's stingy maximum wage.

Within a short period of time players had disposable income and could squander their money on booze, motors, chicks and … drumroll … clothes. Lad culture was born. Instead of getting hitched and hanging up the net curtains, they collectively jumped into the Ford Cortina of life and headed for the nearest boutique.

It would be a mistake to underestimate the impact of fashion on these young blokes who had grown up in the threadbare post-war era. Frank Worthington describes his first trip to Swinging London as a kind of religious experience: 'We'd been saving up for ages in anticipation of splashing out on the latest gear and it was a tremendous feeling knowing that we were just a couple of minutes away from what was then the fashion centre of the World. Carnaby Street was all we had hoped for and more.' Frank came away transformed. My Hall of Fame kicks off on the eve of the Sixties fashion revolution.

Duncan Edwards (1936–1958)

As well as being a sublime sportsman with rugger-bugger legs, Duncan Edwards was also a S-T-A-R. Style, swagger and sizzle, Duncan had it all going on. According to *Guardian* sportswriter Daniel Taylor, Edwards was 'the first player to create the kind of unfettered excitement that George Best, Paul Gascoigne, Ryan Giggs and Wayne Rooney brought later'. But Duncan, bless him, did not live long enough to partake in the Technicolor affluence that exploded in the 1960s. He was one of eight Manchester United players – the 'Busby Babes' – who died in the 1958 Munich air disaster.

Beautiful Duncan, a folk dancer manqué who toyed with becoming a professional morris dancer in his youth, is the perfect kick-off for my footballer fashion Hall of Fame. He is what players looked like before the fashion floodgates opened and turned them all into cologne-wearing poseurs. He is proof that some people don't need designer swag – just as well, since it didn't exist in Duncan's day – in order to shine.

Pelé (Edson Arantes do Nascimento, b. 1940)

Pelé is a mass of contradictions: a short bloke who stands tall; a freewheeling Brazilian who is also deeply religious and views himself as a servant of God; and, finally, a rule-breaking free spirit who, paradoxically, has always cleaved to the establishment.

Was he the greatest? During the 1970 World Cup, a British television commentator asked, 'How do you spell Pelé?' 'Easy: G-O-D', came the response. Regardless of whether Pelé is a deity or not (at the time of writing he is still very much alive and staring down the barrel of 80), he is, and always was, attired to perfection. He looked natty and sharp in the shiny pointy '50s. He gave Steve McQueen-realness in the tight turtleneck-loving '60s. He served up wide-lapelled swagger on the Johnny Carson show in the '70s. When he played for the New York Cosmos, he gave us white-suited Travolta glamour at Studio 54. If 'the Black Pearl' has not earned a place in the footballer fashion Hall of Fame, then nobody has.

'Pelé was one of the few who contradicted my theory: instead of 15 minutes of fame, he will have 15 centuries.'

Andy Warhol

Albert Johanneson (1940–1995)

Lounging in the Wembley stands in 1956, Albert Johanneson cuts a poignant figure. His super-cool, casual appearance lies in sharp contrast to his internal turmoil and sadness. Known as the Black Flash, Johanneson – Leeds United left winger from 1960 to 1970 – was the first black footballer to play in the FA Cup Final. The racial abuse he suffered during his South African childhood, and subsequently in the UK, took a heavy toll on his physical and mental well-being. His rags-to-riches-to-rags story is one of football history's great tear-jerkers. He died alcoholic and unloved in a grim council flat in Leeds, his body remaining undiscovered for days. 'I rise, I rise, I rise', reads the Maya Angelou inscription on his tombstone, an appropriate epitaph for a stylish, talented hero who kicked off football's long, slow odyssey against racism.

Bobby Moore (1941–1993)

'The jumpers in his wardrobe were hung in sequence from dark colours to light', recalled Tina, his gorgeous WAG. A lethal combo of rugged and beauteous, defender Bobby, the blond captain of West Ham, was a stylish bloke who helped popularize the suede trench. He was also, by the way, the footie hero who led the England team to victory in the 1966 World Cup. His bonus? One thousand pounds.

The spectacular World Cup win – which to this 14-year-old felt like the end of the grim, black-and-white post-war years and the dawn of a new age of rampant stylish possibilities – and subsequent attention did not produce enduring benefits for Bobby and Tina. The celebrity machine of agents, PR gurus and brand managers that operates today was not in place. Tina's fame resulted in a spot of modelling and a Bisto gravy ad. Shockingly, Bobby struggled to find a paying gig and subsequently became depressed. He died of cancer at the age of 51.

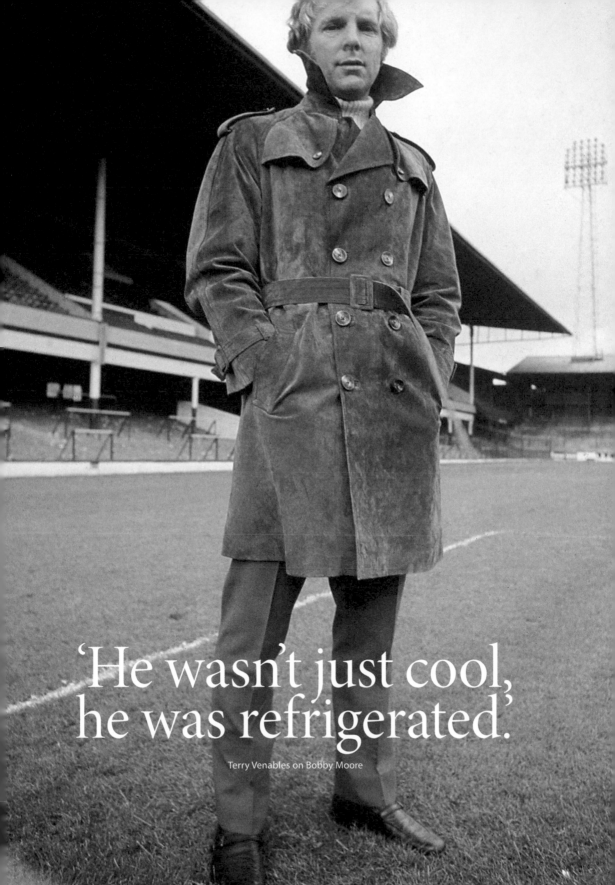

'He wasn't just cool,
he was refrigerated.'

Terry Venables on Bobby Moore

Nobby Stiles (b. 1942)

He was a grunge icon, 30 years before Nirvana hit the charts. The son of a Manchester undertaker, scrawny, scrappy Nobby Stiles is one of the most beloved figures in British football. For every god-like Bobby Moore, there were 500 nutritionally deprived, dentally challenged Nobbys, navigating their way out of austerity Britain.

Nobby played throughout England's triumphant 1966 World Cup campaign, most notably de-fanging the legendary Eusébio in the semi-final against Portugal. We Brits will never forget the sight of Nobby, the anti-Cristiano Ronaldo, holding the World Cup in one hand and his National Health gnashers in the other. Overnight he became the patron saint of denture wearers, which at the time was everyone over the age of 18.

Mike Summerbee (b. 1942)

With the philosophy 'retaliate first', hardman Mike Summerbee played a huge role in Manchester City's dominance in the late 1960s and early 1970s. In the 1968–69 Topical Times annual, Summerbee unleashed his suave side: 'See me roll up in my midnight blue 3-litre Daimler saloon. Out I'll step, wearing one of my expensive suede coats. Cut in the French style I like so much'.

The Best/Summerbee joint-venture boutique mentioned in the Introduction eventually fizzled. George moved on, but Summerbee continued plying his trade, supplying custom shirts to the likes of Michael Caine and David Bowie. Like Best, Buzzer felt that style and glamour were a basic human right.

Günter Netzer (b. 1944)

Gunt, as I like to call him, resembled a combo of Peter Tork of The Monkees and Ray Manzarek of The Doors. Yes, Günter Netzer had it all, by which I of course mean charisma and an astounding mop of tressy blond hair.

A footballing powerhouse with back-to-back Bundesliga triumphs, Günter was voted Footballer of the Year in '72 and '73 and lifted the trophy for West Germany at the '74 World Cup. His accomplishments were huge, as were his shampoo bill and his style quotient. When Barney Ronay declared that this era of the game was epitomized by 'wide-lapel jackets, non-ironical medallions, luxury cars and high-end walnut interiors', he must surely have been thinking about Herr Netzer. Nicknamed Karajan, after Deutschland's flamboyant, equally tressy classical conductor, Herbert von Karajan, Netzer was, along with Best and co., one of the first players to orchestrate an off-field persona. Among his many extramural activities, he ran a nightclub named Lovers' Lane, for which he designed the logo.

'I have an ugly appearance, and long hair inexpressiveness [*sic*] brightens my face, make [*sic*] it a little more attractive.'

Günter Netzer

George Best (1946–2005)

In 2002 Sir Alex Ferguson described George as 'unquestionably the greatest player of all time'. Vulnerable, flawed and gorgeous, George Best is, as I said in my Introduction, the ground zero, the primordial muck from which all fashionable, glamorous, charisma-riddled footballers – the Beckhams, the Gazzas, the Ronaldos – subsequently emerged. Even when he was headed to the FA for a bollocking and a fine, George peacocked his way through the ordeal with the help of velvet and satin and oversized floppy collars.

George's panache was, as Arthur Hopcraft noted, profoundly connected to his exceptional footie genius: 'Seeing him pressing bottles of wine into people's hands at an impromptu party after a match, then stepping jauntily out with a delicious girl in fluffy furs, I was struck by his bravura and his enjoyment of the spotlight. He was not hogging it, but acknowledging its presence while it burned for him. He plays the kind of football he plays because of the kind of person he is.'

Sartorially, George took elements from the far-out counter-culture – velvet, flowery shirts, fringed suede and Black Power turtlenecks – and refined them. In *The Age of Innocence*, Barney Ronay describes the resulting hip/casual style: 'The look for the alpha male footballer of the 1970s was not so much beatnik with a ball as successful Californian advertising executive.' Best's interest in design and style extended beyond the world of clothing. In 1969, 23-year-old George commissioned architect Frazer Crane to build him an ultra-mod house, with a sunken bath and a snooker table being his two main stipulations. The resulting abode on Blossom Lane in Bramhall was every bit as startling and sexy as George himself. Inspired by the lavatorial white brick facade, George's pal, actor Kenny Lynch, changed the name from *Que Sera* to 'the Khazi'.

George's experience of living at the house calls to mind farcical scenes from Jacques Tati's modernist

> 'After training every day he produced shampoo and talcum powder from his washbag and groomed himself as if he was going dancing.'
>
> Eamon Dunphy, recalling teammate Best in his memoir *The Rocky Road*

SIR PAUL SMITH remembers George:

'He was a great bloke, but he did not have the knowledge or experience to be a great retailer, so the boutiques ended up a mess. I would drive up to Manchester to try and sort it out. One night I had worked till midnight, shifting merch around, making displays and trying to make the place look decent, and when it came time to leave I could not figure out how to set the alarm. It went off, very loud. The coppers came. There I was with a Mini parked out front stuffed full of clothes. When I said my name was Smith they pulled out the handcuffs. Eventually we got it sorted. So off I went to George's other shop, and exactly the same thing happened.

Whenever George was missing in action he was in my flat in Putney. Very popular with the girls. I told him, "we're going to put goalposts above your bed because you keep scoring". I tried to help him sort out that ultra-modern Bramhall house. He had installed a huge bath, like the big communal bath in the changing rooms, but this one had a telly at the end. I think George saw himself having baths like Hugh Hefner. Surrounded. But it took too long to fill up. So he never had a bath.'

piss-take movie *Mon Oncle*. 'The guy who designed the house was a bit of a gadget freak, to put it mildly, and almost everything was controlled electronically', recalled George in his autobiography. The various remote-controlled mechanisms were a tad sensitive. Every time a plane flew overhead, 'the curtains started opening and closing, the TV in the lounge began yo-yoing up and down the chimney and the garage door was clanging open and shut'. The fish-bowl house was a magnet for fans who would wave and steal pieces of his lawn. After three years George returned to the arms of Mrs Fullaway, his Chorlton-cum-Hardy landlady.

Sadly, it must be acknowledged that, despite his fame and his instinctive commitment to all things stylish, George was never able to out-run his demons. Those fatal flaws add poignancy to the Best legend. He struggled to the death, and he kept on reworking his look, right to the very end.

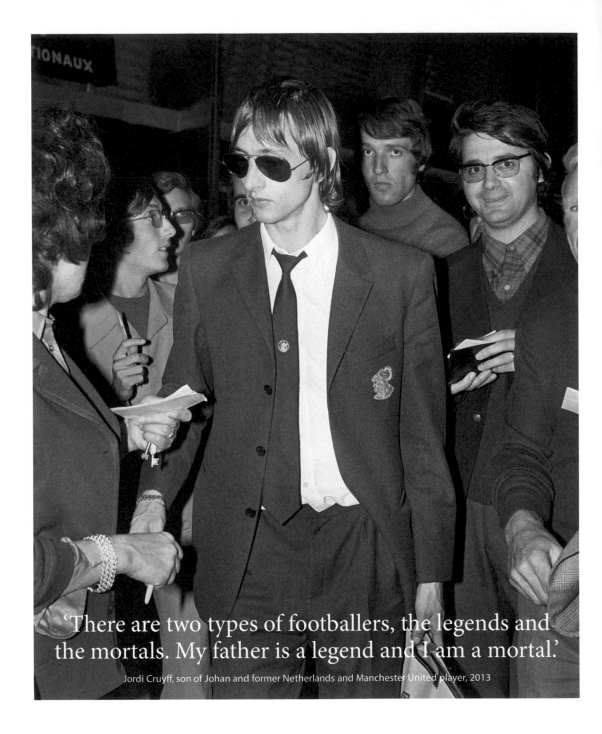

'There are two types of footballers, the legends and the mortals. My father is a legend and I am a mortal.'

Jordi Cruyff, son of Johan and former Netherlands and Manchester United player, 2013

Johan Cruyff (1947–2016)

Johan Cruyff's lifetime accomplishments – king of Total Football, inventor of a signature move named the Cruyff, thrice winner of the Ballon d'Or, Ajax and Barça superstar and manager – were nothing short of insane, but what assures his place in the footballer fashion Hall of Fame are those retro images which forever preserve the memory of his lean and hungry beauty. The lank simplicity of Cruyff's hair, along with his haunted expression, commitment to mirrored aviators and cigarette-smoking, have combined to make him an enduring yardstick for footballer cool.

Alan Hudson (b. 1951)

'Being a player in the '60s and '70s was fantastic fun. We were all young, we followed the fashion scene with a vengeance and were friends with pop stars. Life was far from boring', recalls Hudson, who grew up on the King's Road. Hudson's narrative arc is classic. In 1970 he is photographed showing off his collection of kipper ties; four decades later he is living in a homeless shelter three miles from Stamford Bridge, where he had once played.

Kenny Dalglish (b. 1951)

Julie Burchill wrote of 1970s footballers 'in their three-piece suits, matching ties and clashing cravats, forever peeking cheekily out from under deep fringes'. Celtic and Liverpool icon Kenny Dalglish checks all the boxes.

Kevin Keegan (b. 1951)

Certain footballers, just by virtue of their appearance, can somehow epitomize their particular era. Danny Blanchflower and Jimmy Greaves, for example, were – without ever trying very hard – very, *very* 1950s.

The 1970s was the epoch of hairy hedonism. Despite, or maybe because of the mania for gender-bending rockers and unisex clothing, men have never been more macho and hirsute than they were during those mirrorball years. Piratical swagger was the order of the day. Enter player, manager and almost pop star Kevin Keegan.

Keegan, with his rocker tresses, always looked like he had just crawled out of a man cave. His rugged handsomeness brought him a deluge of spokesman opportunities and licensing deals. 'He was the first British footballer to take hold of the concept of the personal brand', noted Football Supporters' Association founder Rogan Taylor, 'and he managed his way through the jungle that swallowed George Best'.

Malcolm Macdonald (b. 1950)

'I was earning £500 a week and getting mobbed wherever I went. Footballers were the new pop stars and it was all long hair, flares and platform shoes', recalls Malcolm Macdonald, Newcastle's fifth highest goalscorer of all time.

Robin Friday (1952–1990)

Robin Friday had jutting cheekbones, long hair and a short life. He was what you might call *creatively impulsive*. He once picked up a swan and carried it into a bar. Robin played for Reading – he was the most exciting, hedonistic, spotlight-grabbing player ever to grace Elm Park – so he is very close to my heart. In addition to being a spotlight-grabber, he was also a testicle-grabber. Even Bobby Moore once experienced 'the Hand of Friday'.

Mr Friday broke all the rules of footballer fashion. Players were not supposed to dress like Paul Rodgers, Eric Clapton or Jimmy Page, but Robin Friday, in his Afghan coat from Kensington Market, gave it a whirl. His wedding, to a nice Reading girl named Liza, was filmed by Southern Television. Wearing snakeskin boots, a brown velvet suit and an open-necked tiger-print shirt, Robin sat down on the church steps, in front of the media, and rolled a joint. Drinking, drugging and fighting were the order of the day; after nicking the couple's wedding presents, Robin's two hundred or so closest friends staggered back to London.

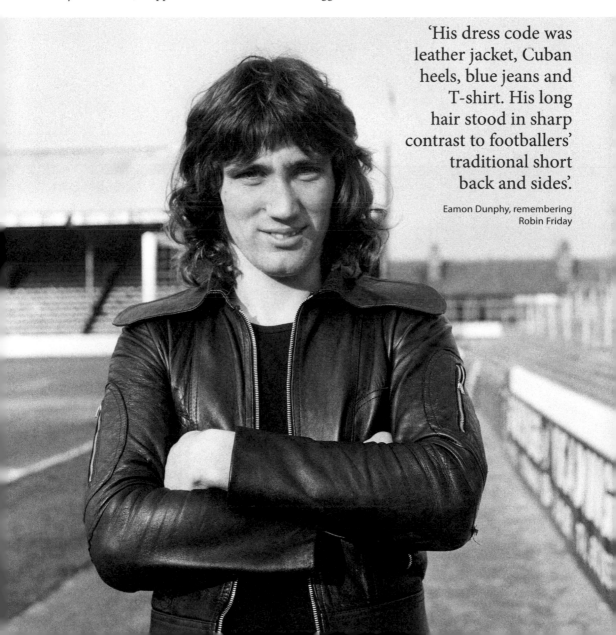

'His dress code was leather jacket, Cuban heels, blue jeans and T-shirt. His long hair stood in sharp contrast to footballers' traditional short back and sides'.

Eamon Dunphy, remembering Robin Friday

The Three Degrees: Brendon Batson (b. 1953), Laurie Cunningham (1956–1989) and Cyrille Regis (1958–2018)

In the late 1970s there were only about fifty black players in the British game. Then, suddenly, there were three more: in the 1977/78 season Brendon Batson, Laurie Cunningham and Cyrille Regis joined West Bromwich Albion. Manager Ron Atkinson nicknamed his smoking hot trio the Three Degrees, in homage to the eponymous chart-topping chanteuses (pictured above). 'They could have been yellow, purple and have two heads, so long as they could play and they were good lads – and they were', roared Big Ron. The media vigorously embraced this powerful moment of black pride. The fans? Not so much. 'What shocked me when I joined West Brom was the volume', remembered Batson in *The Guardian*. 'The noise and level of the abuse was incredible … We'd get off the coach at away matches and the National Front would be right there in your face. In those days, we didn't have security and we'd have to run the gauntlet. We'd get to the players' entrance and there'd be spit on my jacket or Cyrille's shirt. It was a sign of the times. I don't recall making a big hue and cry about it. We coped. It wasn't a new phenomenon to us.'

Charlie Nicholas (b. 1961)

In the 1980s, football entered what *Soccernomics* co-authors Simon Kuper and Stefan Szymanski call the Dark Ages: 'The combination of decrepit stadiums and hooliganism provoked an existential crisis.' Between 1978 and 1989, attendance at British games fell by 41 per cent.

Though the 1980s were economically grim, the players' passionate commitment to the finer things in life – getting rat-arsed as often as possible and blowing insane amounts of cash on motors, gambling, chicks and whistles – continued unabated. Enter Arsenal's Charlie Nicholas, an improbable fashion influencer. With his Wham! haircut, fashion-forward leather trousers and dangling earring, Charlie spawned legions of lookalike fans.

Charlie had an open-plan pad in Highgate. Paul Merson dropped by and had his mind well and truly blown: 'Tears for Fears and Howard Jones blasted out from the speakers. I looked like the character Garth from *Wayne's World* because my eyes kept locking onto every passing set of pins like heat-seeking radar.' In 1995 Charlie sought to correct misperceptions about his social life during his Arsenal years with a weighty public statement: 'People reckon I spent all my time in Stringfellows but I never went there that much. I preferred Tramp.'

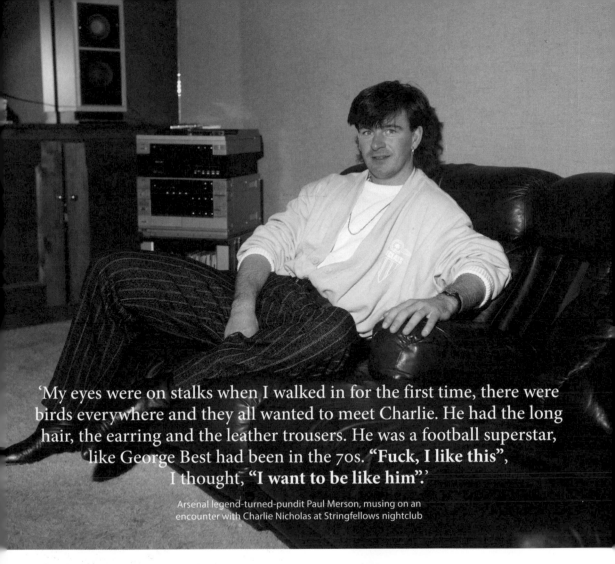

'My eyes were on stalks when I walked in for the first time, there were birds everywhere and they all wanted to meet Charlie. He had the long hair, the earring and the leather trousers. He was a football superstar, like George Best had been in the 70s. **"Fuck, I like this"**, I thought, **"I want to be like him".**'

Arsenal legend-turned-pundit Paul Merson, musing on an encounter with Charlie Nicholas at Stringfellows nightclub

Will Frears, writer/director and lifelong Arsenal supporter, recalls the galvanizing fashion influence of Charlie Nicholas:

'At home in North London my mum has two pictures of me, aged ten and eleven. In the first, taken in 1983, I am wearing Clarks shoes, cords, and a grey sweatshirt with my hair in a modified bowl cut. The second was taken just one year later, but I am transformed: electric blue Nikes, baggies (loose-fit blue jeans with lots of zips), a striped Sergio Tacchini jumper with a prominent logo. My hair is cut long in the back, short and parted on the top, and slightly shaved at the sides. The back is only not permed because my mother forbade it, and she was still paying. Charlie Nicholas had come to Arsenal. The awakening was in effect.'

Eric Cantona (b. 1966)

Enigma, sage, thespian, philosopher ('It is enjoyable to make things visible which are invisible'), spectator-chopper – the former Manchester United #7 forward is a whole lot of things, but hardly a fashion peacock. Cantona makes it into the Hall of Fame because he was, and remains, a total original. Lots of footie players look like other footie players. Not Cantona. His dour, curmudgeonly mien is unique, and has made him an enduring fashion icon.

> 'I have to wear clothes but I don't like to give an idea of what I am [*sic*] with clothes'.
>
> Eric Cantona

Tony Adams (b. 1966)

Arsenal great Tony Adams's fearless memoir, *Addicted*, includes many insightful recollections of his fashion odyssey. Of the 1970s, he writes: 'When the mod revival began in the late '70s I bought a Parka coat and Hush Puppies and thought I looked really smart. It always appealed to me more than the rocker and Greaser stuff.' Of the 1980s: 'I was a soul boy, into jazz funk, which was not very fashionable out in Essex.' And of the 1990s, when serving the four-month sentence he received after smashing his Ford Sierra into a wall while blotto (of which he served 57 days): 'Then I was issued with prison wear: dark blue jeans, which I later doodled on with a pen, a sky-blue T-shirt, a tatty woollen pullover which was too tight, blue socks and black plimsolls.'

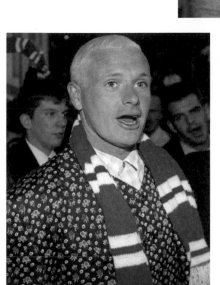

'I was wearing one of my daft suits, a brand new Armani outfit in some garish colour.'

Paul Gascoigne, recalling his attire on the occasion when Rangers manager Walter Smith attempted to throttle him

Paul Gascoigne (b. 1967)

Paul Gascoigne is one of the most beloved figures in the history of football. Having grown up poor in Gateshead, when he made some dough he understandably developed a pools-winner mentality. Like a male Viv Nicholson he spent, spent, spent: 'I went out and bought ten Versace suits – but in all the brightest colours … and I got my hair bleached. I can't remember why. It must have seemed like a good idea at the time.'

His playing record – among his triumphs he won 57 caps and scored ten goals for England – is nothing short of astounding. Despite his craziness, Gazza is truly adored. David Beckham explained: 'Once you've played in the same side as Gazza you fall in love with him because of the sort of person he is.' As Michael Caine put it: 'Gazza reminds me of Marilyn Monroe. She wasn't the greatest actress in the world, but she was a star and you didn't mind if she was late.'

David Ginola (b. 1967)

Footballers are a good-looking bunch, but some are so romance-novel handsome that it's scary. Enter French international turned actor and pundit, David Ginola. As former England midfielder Chris Waddle put it in 1995, 'Men will love his skills and women his looks. He could end up being popular enough to replace Robbie Williams in Take That.'

Monsieur Ginola appears acutely aware of his beauty, even in middle age. On 14 May 2017, after Tottenham Hotspur played their last game at White Hart Lane, David was invited to join the heart-warming parade of former Spurs legends at the post-game ceremony. Ginola, the suavely attired peacock, was the only bloke who strode into the roaring historic stadium while filming *himself*.

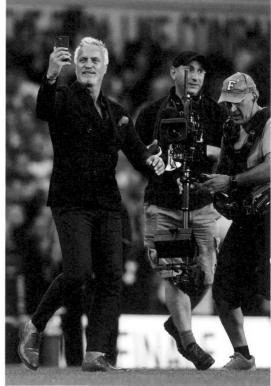

David Beckham (b. 1975)

If George Best was football fashion's first brave apostle, then David Beckham is surely its most triumphant and splendid apotheosis. Either way, stylish Georgie was a lovely warm-up for the tour de force and global style-yardstick that is David Robert Joseph Beckham OBE.

Both Becks and Best displayed, at a young age, a spontaneous, instinctive interest in trendy clobber. Especially Beckham. Aged seven he was prancing round the house in a Little Lord Fauntleroy outfit with a frilly shirt and velvet knickers. The ensemble in question had been purchased for a family wedding, but David incorporated it into his daily wardrobe. Hairdresser mum Sandra warned him he risked

derision, but he simply did not care. In other parallels, Becks and Best both experienced – and enjoyed – a stratospheric level of notoriety that propelled them beyond the footie universe. Cultural touchstones, you might say. Plus both lads wore the #7 for Manchester United (Cristiano Ronaldo also wore the #7 at Man U, making a footie-fashion troika).

Timing was key for the trajectories of both Best and Becks: George hit the crest of the Swinging Sixties and became part of it. David's timing was no less significant. It was, in fact, almost ridiculously *more* significant. The pre-millennium football landscape was filled with dissolute, dark, troubled geniuses; then along came Beckham, a handsome, high-functioning milk-drinking romantic prince, a messenger of positivity and light. Beckham grew up in the shadow of lads like George who had messed up their lives with drink, some ending up on benefits and/or living with mum. Beckham re-wrote the script.

Beckham's arrival coincided with major cultural shifts. First, this was the era when fashion was becoming FASHION, a global, throbbing, screeching, Sex-and-the-City, shimmering spectator sport. The increasing interest in fashion was paralleled by an even greater, infinitely more annoying phenomenon: the return of celebrity culture. Around this time somebody opened Pandora's box – we should try to find out who it was and put them on trial for crimes against humanity – and the old obsession with red carpets and fame and gossip came roaring back into our culture.

But, wait, there's more: Beckham's ascent also coincided with the birth of the Premier League. In fact, he started at Man Utd in 1992, the formation year of the Premier League. Football, with its newly minted media partners and sponsorship deals, had never been more cash-drenched, tantalizing, televised and generally zhooshy. It was a perfect storm: fashion + celebrity + tv + shekels + a great-looking, talented lad from Leytonstone who looked perfect in whatever he wore and whose only questionable habits seemed to be a penchant for folding towels (fun fact: Don Revie and Paul Gascoigne were/are also obsessive towel-folders).

Beckham's unbridled consumption of cars, fashion, scented candles and new haircuts made George Best look like Mahatma Gandhi, and paved the way for Posh and Becks to become the most talked-about couple in the universe. For those of us who grew up in the Dagenhams, Grimsbys and Readings of the world, and were desperate for a way out, Posh and Becks' drive makes perfect sense. Success, aspiration, money … why not? These are good things. Becks got rich doing something he enjoys. Ditto Victoria. They inspire envy because they achieved success through their own efforts doing things they enjoy. As Julie Burchill notes in her charming little tome *Burchill on Beckham*, the Beckhams 'never took a penny from the public that was not willingly proffered'.

Left The skirt that was heard around the world.

Above Which way to the Emma Peel lookalike contest?

'I like nice clothes whether they are dodgy or not.'

David Beckham

The Beckham phenomenon resulted in many iconic fashion tableaux. Two in particular stand out. What to wear for a night out with your fiancée during the 1998 France World Cup? How about a black sleeveless V-neck, a wide-legged pant and a sarong? What's sarong with that? Then one year later, not long after their fairytale wedding (at which the couple sat on gold thrones and Victoria wore a crown), came the his'n'hers kinky black leather moment. The married couple showed up at a Versace store opening wearing Gucci outfits, *which they had purchased themselves at full retail*. I look back upon these innocent expressions of fun and fabulosity with misty nostalgia. The reckless spontaneity of Posh and Becks calls to us from the era before social media came along and ruined everything. Nowadays the gun-shy celebs think twice before doing, saying or wearing anything playful or unconventional.

July 2001. David Beckham appears on the cover of *The Face*, the now-extinct bible of fashion esoterica, thereby achieving something unprecedented for a footballer: fashion-insider legitimacy. No longer just a consumer of clothing and a popularizer of blokey trends, he is a bona fide inspirational icon of cool. In the subsequent decade Beckham took his cool and his fashion legitimacy and made it into a brand that, five years after his retirement, is still cha-chinging at the cash registers.

Though classic in his tastes, Beckham has, in recent years, dramatically increased his repertoire of styles. Depending on the hour and location, he might well serve up any of the following: bespoke businessman Beckham, Motocross Beckham, hipster-dad Beckham, *Ocean's Eleven* white tux Beckham, and last but not least, happily-flaunting-it-in-your-undies Beckham. As Julie Burchill noted, 'it is obviously Beckham's sexual confidence which has kept him so singularly sane and happy.'

Postscript: it's a relief to discover that not everything about Beckham is so fabulously fashionable. When Zlatan Ibrahimović and Becks were playing together at Paris Saint-Germain, the former snooped in the latter's playlist and found 'lots of Justin Bieber, Jonas Brothers and Selena Gomez. We were expecting some cool English rock bands and hip hop. It's nice to know even David Beckham doesn't have good taste in everything.'

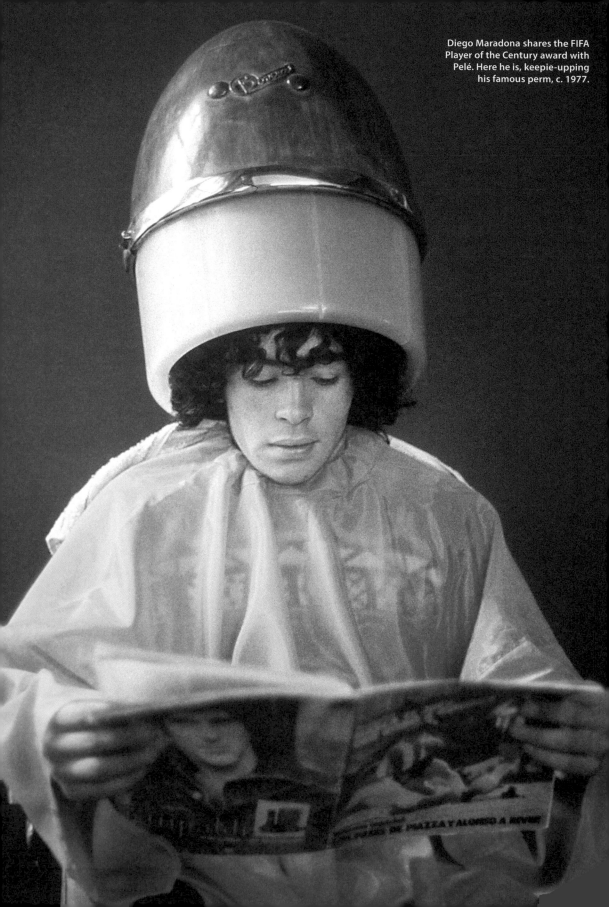

Diego Maradona shares the FIFA Player of the Century award with Pelé. Here he is, keepie-upping his famous perm, c. 1977.

> 'One reason he's improved so much is **he's stopped messing about with his barnet.**'
>
> Spurs manager Harry Redknapp on Gareth Bale, 2010

3. Bleach It Like Beckham

The Hairdos and Don'ts of Footie History

Football managers loathe any and all expressions of trendy flamboyance, and areas of concern extend way beyond the players' dodgy clothing choices. More often than not, it is the players' hairstyles – those bloody barnets! – which are causing life-threatening spikes in manager blood pressure.

Dressing 'funny' and acting stupid are synonymous in the manager brain, but at least those trendy clothes are discarded and shoved inside a dressing-room locker. Trendy hairdos? They fly around the pitch, taunting, mocking and throwing the finger at all and sundry.

In the early days it was all about length. Back in the 1960s, Tottenham's Bill Nicholson regularly inveighed against long hair ('It sickened me'), and nothing made him more irate than the sound of that womanly and devilish totem, the hairdryer. Over time, the focus of contention shifted from hair length, with all its connotations of girliness and rebellion, to hairstyle innovation.

Barcelona-born Héctor Bellerín had a surprise attack of the cornrows at the FA Cup semi-final in 2017.

Disgust at trendy new hairstyles has become part of footie lore – Sir Alex Ferguson's Battle of Barnet with Beckham being the best known. When Fergie saw the mohawk that Beckham acquired in preparation for his 2001 *Face* magazine cover photo shoot, he blew a gasket. Beckham held his ground. Fergie gave him a Voldemort glare. Beckham ran into the bog and shaved it off. 'He felt it wasn't the right look. We were playing at Wembley too, so he kind of had a point', reminisced the affable style god on *The Graham Norton Show* in 2015.

'We want football players, not fashion models', ranted then Chelsea manager José Mourinho in 2013, adding, 'Last year Kevin-Prince Boateng had more hairstyles than goals.' Given the withering critiques doled out by managers, and considering how much lacerating social media feedback players receive every time they unveil a new style, it is nothing short of a bloody miracle they do anything other than simply shave their heads. Seemingly oblivious to all the negative feedback, footballers continue to adopt and discard ever more provocative hairdos. Managers may scold, haters may vent, but a significant number of fans are rushing to the barber shop and screeching 'I want the new Agüero/Hamšík/Firmino!' Footie players are nothing if not influential. Legions of young supporters think nothing of chopping and changing and bleaching their locks in a frenzied attempt to keep pace with the changing styles of their idols. The footie hair landscape, at first glance so diverse and demented, can be simplified and broken down into some clear and fabulous categories.

Middlesbrough winger Adama Traoré having a blond moment in 2017. It's hard to tell if he's having more fun.

The 2016/17 season. A tidal wave of wicked peroxide engulfs the world of footie: Antoine Griezmann, Phil Jones, Lionel Messi, Samir Nasri and Aaron Ramsey (pictured, right) each reached for the bleach.

Bottle blonds

Peroxide is synonymous with loose morals, homicidal superfreaks and barmaids in leopard-print halter tops. Nice girls do not bleach their hair. And nice boys? Naturally blond choirboys and sun-bleached surfer-dudes embody virtue and idealism respectively. But male bottle blonds? Send in the punks, the Bond villains and the footballers, the bad boys of bleach.

Very occasionally, something shifts in the cosmos and the lads go blond in groups. Liverpool players Robbie Fowler, David James, Dominic Matteo et al. formed their own blond cult while on holiday in 1995. The ultimate group-peroxide pact occurred at the '98 World Cup. For their match against Tunisia the entire Romanian team hit the bleach. The effect was creepy rather than celebratory, recalling the movie *Village of the Damned*. The score? A haunting 1:1 draw.

0kcal

Beckham, tousled and frosted, giving us just a smidgen of Blue Steel.

Frosted tips

Frosting and highlighting require commitment and dedication. In order to achieve that sunkissed-in-Ibiza look, many players – Torres, Behrami, Coentrão and, of course, Pogba and Neymar – sit for hours listening to Taylor Swift while their top-notch hairdressers meticulously apply mini-bleaching foils to their tufts.

Danish national forward Nicklas Bendtner, proving that there is nothing more poignant than a man bun which has not quite happened yet.

Adored by women, envied and mocked by men, the man bun, like Gareth Bale's, is a coiffure lightning rod.

Man buns

Zlatan Ibrahimović, Andy Carroll, Gareth Bale and Dani 'Pablo' Osvaldo are the current reigning man-bun kings. Watford defender Sebastian Prödl is, like many players across the globe, currently attempting to grow one. Caution: a man bun needs ten to twelve inches of hair. With a growth rate of half an inch per month, your hair will require a two-year advanced warning.

Zlatan Ibrahimović's man bun is iconic and courageous. I say courageous because man buns are a young man's game and Zlat is no longer in the first flush of youth. At 36 years old, he is staring down the end of his man-bun years. Why? Two words that strike terror into the heart of any footballer: Traction alopecia. Yanking your hair off your face into a warrior man bun lifts loose skin and flatters the bone structure, *but it also accelerates hair loss.*

HAIRY HE-MEN OF YORE

Where the wild things are. Hairy Sheffield United icons Trevor Hockey and Tony Currie – the latter of the famous Currie/Birchenall kiss – rocking their thundering thatches.

Match of the Day, April 1975. Sheffield United were playing Leicester City. The Brit population gasped when, after colliding on the pitch, Tony Currie and Alan Birchenall, sitting side by side, suddenly puckered up and kissed each other. It was a real Madonna-and-Britney cultural moment. Looking at photos of the incident now, it's not the kiss that shocks, it's the hair, and the astounding amount thereof. The massive leonine tresses sported by players in the 1970s are far more shocking than any laddish lip-lock.

The 1970s and 1980s were the golden age of footie follicles. George Best raised the bar and everyone followed. Looking at images of these astoundingly hairy players – Mike Flanagan, Bob Latchford, Pat Jennings, Jerzy Gorgoń, Alan Hudson, Günter Netzer – and comparing them with players today, one starts to wonder if people actually had thicker hair back then. Or maybe thinning scissors had yet to be invented.

Charlie George's uncontrived '70s bad-boy coiffure was much copied and remains part of Arsenal's history. Charlie was a local Islington-born lad who grew up on the Highbury terraces. Recalls Nick Hornby: 'His long, lank hair remained unfeathered and unlayered, right up until the time he unwisely decided upon a bubble perm from hell some time in the mid-seventies.' In fairness to the George legacy, we should remind ourselves just how many high-profile players elected to perm their way out of the '70s: Maradona, Keegan and Derek Possee, Millwall's third highest all-time goalscorer, each traded in their silky tresses for the dodgy 'dandelion' look.

By the 1990s longer hair, with its inherent faffing complications, is on the way out. Once in a while a reckless player adopts a tressier style, but things invariably end in tragedy. In 1993 Paul Merson decided on 'a slightly windswept style that had become the height of fashion at the time'. For reasons best known to himself, the hairdresser threw a perm into the mix, with terrifying results: 'Rather than looking like Brad Pitt', recalled Merson, 'I looked like Cher after a night on the razz.'

Paul Breitner and Kevin Keegan enjoy a Bundesliga Barnet-off in Hamburg, c. 1979.

Charlie George's limp locks were legendary.

'CHARLIE GEORGE! SUPERSTAR! HE WALKS LIKE A WOMAN AND HE WEARS A BRA!'

Chant delivered by opposing fans, in response to the Arsenal chant, 'Charlie George! Superstar! How many goals have you scored so far?'

Chris Waddle flaunting a stylized '80s mullet during the 1990 World Cup. The score: England 1, Belgium 0.

Man City defender Nicolás Otamendi puts his cockatiel to good use.

The cockatiel

Coutinho, Lallana, Agüero, Negredo and Giroud are enthusiastic proponents. It's not a fauxhawk. It's less than a Hollywood pompadour and so much more than a toilet brush. It's a militaristic short back and sides, with an erect flourish on top. It's the cockatiel, the most popular hairdo in football.

An important issue to consider before going cockatiel is head-shape. According to my barber, Mr Johnny Gaita of New York City, 'Pea-heads can be challenging, but the worst is guys with giant pan-heads. It ends up looking like a toupée resting on a beach ball.'

Liverpool goalie Loris Karius wins points for giving the top of his undercut a light bleaching, thereby accentuating the textural difference between the undercut's floppy top and the shorn sides.

The undercut

When footie players tire of their cockatiels and look to evolve, the undercut is the logical next step. All you have to do is tell your barber to keep shaving the back and sides but to leave the top alone for a few months. Eventually the upper tress will reach an impressive uniform length. Proponents of the undercut include Spurs central defender and occasional right back Toby Alderweireld, Leicester City winger Riyad Mahrez, Shandong Luneng striker Graziano Pellè, Sevilla forward Nolito and actress Tilda Swinton.

How do undercuts stay so relentlessly intact and immobile, even during a soggy, violent game? Online speculation is rife. Alderweireld in particular is regularly deluged with fan requests for info regarding his choice of unguent, such is the majesty and staying power of his undercut. I cannot help but feel that there is a hair-gunk licensing deal in his future.

The footpath

The shaved sides and rear of any style can be personalized and enhanced with the addition of lines and zigzags. Spurs winger/midfielder Erik 'Coco' Lamela has enhanced his cropped mohawk with many a footpath. Man City's Agüero, like his former playmate Negredo, is no stranger to these graphic design elements. Ditto Man U's Paul Pogba. Liverpool's Sadio Mané adds racing-stripe dynamism by bleaching a winding trail on the side of his head.

Warning: don't try it at home. Carving footpaths – not to mention racing stripes, lightning bolts and stars – into one's shorn follicles is specialized work. Players like Wayne Rooney, Gareth Bale and Mario Balotelli rely on superstar barbers like Watford-based legend Daniel Johnson.

Most footie players have flaunted the occasional footpath. Only Man City central defender Vincent Kompany has replicated the map of an entire housing estate.

Ready for anything: Benoît Assou-Ekotto arrives at the Spurs training ground in 2011 sporting a magnificently elaborate do.

Crystal Palace winger Wilfried Zaha showing off his Afro-cockatiel. Also favoured by Man City midfielder Raheem Sterling, this do emphasizes the killer cheekbones and massively expressive eyes of both players.

Afro-magic

Low-fades, high-tops, casual crops, curly-fades, waved, coiled or kinky box-fades, straight-across short-fades etc., etc.: the magnificent history of black hair is on display whenever Saturday comes. Sturridge, Lukaku, Rashford, Mikel, Walker, Rose, Benteke, Bailly, Sissoko, Townsend … the list of black players with noteworthy and diverse haircuts is staggering.

In addition to the classic barber-shop styles, there is no shortage of explosive Afro-creativity. Black hair is about dynamic styling and even more dynamic restyling. Beaded, braided, cornrowed, shaved or coloured, the ever-changing majesty of Balotelli, Pogba, Yedlin, Sagna, Leroy Sané, Jason Lee, Nile Ranger, Gervinho and various Ninjas and Assassins, past and present, consistently add creativity and dynamism to the footie landscape.

In clothing, music and hair, black style is the dominant source of inspiration in our culture. Small wonder, then, that so many white players, from Gazza to Beckham, Andy Carroll to Héctor Bellerín, have made stylistic pilgrimages to the hood, appropriating cornrows and dreads with varying degrees of success.

Napoli attacking midfielder Marek Hamšík sports a mohawk style that is clearly intended to shrivel the nads of any opponent.

The mohawk

Whether it's a fauxhawk, a curly hawk, a psychobilly deathhawk or your basic Hoxton fin, the mohawk has one goal: INTIMIDATION. Scythian warriors, World War II GIs, King's Road punks, not to mention the Mohicans who gave name to the do, have all wielded this fearsome style.

Though insanely diverse, footballer mohawks have one basic limitation: scale. Cartwheel mohawks – I am thinking of those punk-rock extravaganzas, comparable in diameter to the London Eye – are high maintenance and require an enormous amount of gunk in order to maintain their erections. Firing a penalty shoot-out at Camp Nou on a boiling Spanish Saturday with five pounds of egg white, gelatin and corn starch coursing down your face is nobody's idea of a good time. As a result, the shorter fauxhawk and the 'fro-hawk remain the footballer favourites.

A rainbow of follicles

Colour, in the world of football, is loaded with incendiary potential. Exuberant fans frequently colour their hair in order to taunt opposing fans. Colourful coiffures on players, however, are somewhat rare and exquisite.

Martín Mantovani's sky-blue cockatiel matched his kit, and surely helped propel CD Leganés from the Spanish third division into La Liga. Paul Scharner gave us electric-blue flashes. Freddie Ljungberg has dabbled with sapphire blue, but is also no stranger to imperial purple and raging magenta. Nigerian Taribo West gave good green and Kevin Kampl indulged in a shocking-pink situation. Colours come and go, but the one thing you can always count on is that Paul Pogba, Manchester United's highly compensated Psychedelic Ninja, will sing a rainbow on a regular basis. So identified is the midfielder with colourful flashes that when, in 2017, fellow French national and Chelsea midfielder Bakayoko dyed his locks 'blue-is-the-colour' Chelsea blue, he was accused by pundits of 'doing a Pogba'.

Brazilian striker Vágner Love: the blue braids match his blue vibe. Cheer up, luv.

Chelsea defender David Luiz attempts to style his signature profusion of curls.

HAIRY HE-MEN OF TODAY

Andrea Pirlo, recently the owner of the most celebrated long hair in the world of footie.

A couple of years back, Everton's Leighton Baines did a valiant job of excavating that groovy '70s Alan Hudson/Rod Stewart hairstyle: lengthy phalanges at the back and side and short on top. It did not last, nor did it catch on. The reasons? As Liam Gallagher can no doubt attest, It takes a long time to grow it, and many hours to comb, arrange and spray it. The look is ace, but this style, on the pitch, is a maintenance nightmare. One gust of wind and suddenly you resemble your aunt Brenda after she fell off her bicycle.

Foaming tresses are few and far between in today's Premier League. Burnley midfielder Jeff Hendrick and Sheffield Wednesday winger George Boyd – the latter deploys a wide black supermodel headband – are about as good as it gets. Today's players, with their low-maintenance precision cuts, are disinclined to spend time farting around with their hair – in today's world, farting around with one's hair has been replaced by farting around with one's phone. Shame, really. If you are searching for hairy manes, you need to cross the pond to the MLS, where follicles roam free, and the culture of designer dandyism, cockatiels, footpaths and mohawks has yet to acquire a stranglehold.

Andrea Pirlo, who played for New York City FC before his recent retirement, is one of the greatest hairy hair icons of all time. With 116 appearances, Pirlo is the fourth most-capped player in the history of the Italian national team. In April 2016, 3,000 New York City fans voted in the club's Hair Madness challenge. Pirlo, and his effortlessly perfect mop, snagged 67 per cent of the votes, defeating seven-seed David Villa. 'It's the best hair', purred Pirlo, 'because it's mine'.

Baldies

Many of the twentieth century's most iconic players struggled with comb-overs rather than taking the seemingly easier route of head-shaving. Why? In Sir Bobby Charlton's straggly heyday, shaved heads were viewed as being *very* unsavoury. Only convicts and people with lice infestations shaved their heads. For players in the 1980s, shaving carried the additional stigma of the Skinheads.

Things started to change in the 1990s. When Freddie Ljungberg shaved his head, he proved that bald is beautiful and ushered in a glorious post-comb-over world. Shaved heads came to signify power and a mysterious invincibility. Footballers like Merson and Beckham sought to imbue themselves with superhuman strength by shearing *off* their locks. Call it the Un-Samson effect.

While analyzing today's footie hair scene, I noticed a strange baldie cluster phenomenon. For example: Millwall's only baldie, at the time of writing, is Nadjim Abdou. West Ham, on the other hand, has a veritable baldie-fest that includes André Ayew, Angelo Ogbonna, James Collins and Pablo Zabaleta. And don't get me started on Man City: Kompany, Mendy, Delph, Silva, Mangala and Fernandinho, not to mention manager Pep Guardiola, are proud and handsome baldies, one and all. I suspect there may be a conformity dynamic at play in the dressing room: *'ere, can I borrow your clippers?*

'One day, we lost a game and I got really angry and I shaved my head. I had just signed an endorsement with a hair product company and I lost it the next day. And that's how I am bald even today.'

Arsenal and Sweden legend, Freddie Ljungberg

VANITY FAIR: BEAUTY TIPS FROM FOOTIE WORLD

MANSCAPING

'Footballers are turning into women. You'd never have got away with anything like that when I was playing.'

Gordon Ramsay in 2005, responding to reports that top players were shaving their body hair

LOVE HANDLES

'It's just water and lemon plus a bit of maple syrup for energy. I throw a bit of cayenne pepper into it to give it some sort of taste. I drink four litre bottles a day, all day long, for four days. On the fourth day I'll have a chicken sandwich.'

Paul Gascoigne outlining his personal diet in his 2004 autobiography

BABIES' BOTTOMS

'When I played, my mate John Fashanu said, "Jonesy, you've got to moisturize – you'll thank me when you're older". So I've been moisturizing for 20 years and it's paid off. When I have a shave, my skin is very soft.'

Vinnie Jones, former Wales captain and now an actor in Los Angeles, 2013

PLUGS

'Just to confirm to all my followers I have had a hair transplant. I was going bald at 25. Why not?'

Wayne Rooney on Twitter, 2011

SPRITZING

'I always spray perfume on my shirt before we play. The other guys are happy with it because they know I smell good when we celebrate.'

Florent Malouda, former Chelsea and France midfielder, 2010

KICKING IT OLD-SCHOOL

'My gran uses it so why not?'

Beckham extolling Elnett hairspray in *People* magazine, 2015

STATURE

'I owe Barcelona everything because they paid for my growth-hormone treatment.'

Lionel Messi showing gratitude in 2007

Beards – the hipster invasion?

There has always been an undisguised antipathy in football towards beards. The working-class ethos that underpins the game was at odds with the CND bearded peaceniks and hippies of the last century. This attitude persisted into the twentieth century ... until now.

Scruff came first. Starting around 2013, cockatiels and mini-hawks were increasingly balanced out with shadowy facial hair. Swansea City, for example, had multiple scruffers, including Amat, Taylor, Bastón, Dyer, Birighitti and Nordfeldt, who grew a full beard. Before long more beards followed: Ledley of Crystal Palace, Snodgrass of Hull City, Jedinak of Aston Villa and Agüero and Otamendi of Man City.

On 10 December 2016 I tuned in to watch Arsenal at home to Stoke. As soon as the lads emerged from the tunnel, I saw that something was clearly amiss. A quick overview of both teams yielded the following shocking stats: 19 out of 35 Stoke players had grown beards. Arsenal? Over 50 per cent of the players were fully bearded. Within a very short space of time beards have become ubiquitous, and Olivier Giroud has started to resemble Dostoevsky.

Breaking news! Man grows beard.

65

Dutch national Memphis Depay, an Aquarius, displays his leonine side.

> 'Perhaps, as football becomes more athletic and players skinnier, [tattooing] provides atavistic reassurance **they're still warriors.**'
>
> Alex Anderson in *When Saturday Comes* magazine

4. Ink

The Poetry, the Platitudes and the Pain

According to the FDA more than 45 million Americans are now tattooed. In the UK it's a staggering 20 million, one in three young adults. Footballers? These days you would be hard pressed to find a tattoo-free inch of footballer flesh.

Having, one assumes, run out of upper torso space, German-Ghanaian midfielder Kevin-Prince Boateng just enlivened his upper thighs with large tragic/comic masks. Herr Boateng and ex-Newcastle striker Nile Ranger have even resorted to tattooing the insides of their mouths. WHY?

Just as with psycho barnets, tattoos offer players opportunities for rebellion and unbridled self-expression. *You can stuff me into a blazer and flannels but you can't stop me emblazoning my back with poems, snarling wolves and ghouls.* But there's more. Tattoos kill time. Lying on your face for hours while some dude enlivens your epidermis with skulls and Sanskrit seems, at first glance, like a reckless waste of time. But footballers have nothing but time, what with those long post-training afternoon voids – so online gambling, Playstation and tattooing to the rescue!

Then there's the dosh: most tattoo artists charge about $150 per hour. A full sleeve can take 40 hours. Bingo! $6000, plus another $6000 for laser removal when you hit late middle age and it's gone all crepey – no longer recognizable as a dragon but looking more like a squashed squirrel. You went from being the bloke with the dragon tattoo to the old git with the squashed squirrel, and it only cost you the deposit on a house. But footie players have nothing but dough, burning a hole in the pockets of their ripped designer jeans.

And then there's the masochism. Arsenal forward Theo Walcott has many tattoos, including a mysterious lady wrapped in goblins on his left arm. Speaking to the Arsenal website, Theo is candid about the pleasure he experiences during his sessions with footballer favourite Louis Molloy: 'I like the sensation of it ... I did an eight and a half hour sitting, but again, I like the feel of it.' There are even more compelling reasons why players choose to tattoo themselves, but I will save these for the end of this chapter: let's get to the ink.

They say the eyes are the windows to the soul. I believe – and I will prove to you – that body ink, not pupils and irises, provides a much clearer portal into the footballer soul. Tattoos certainly reveal more than anything that might come out of a footballer's mouth. Consider for a moment those guarded post-match interviews. Today's media-trained players skilfully burp up those boilerplate comments without revealing a thing. *You get nothing.* But check out the ink. Just read the tattoos, and the murkiest corners of the player psyche are instantly revealed. Here, for your edification, are just some of the deep psychological insights that I have gleaned from a careful examination of footballer ink.

Players get homesick

Transplanted footballers frequently experience feelings of wistful melancholy. Don't mock. If you had to leave sunny Seville for rain-lashed Ancoats, you might also experience the occasional mood swing. Clubs attempt to ease these transitions by employing professional relocation consultants. But the players are also doing their bit to combat relocation depression, via tattoos. What better way to counteract homesickness than to contemplate images of one's home-town monuments? And why would you Google-image those iconic monuments when you

can have them painstakingly inked onto your body?

On Aaron Ramsey's right leg you will find a touching depiction of Caerphilly Castle, along with St Michael and other symbols of Welshness. In a similar vein – and quite possibly *on* a similar vein – Raul Meireles, the Portuguese Psychedelic Ninja, expresses a passionate nostalgia for the sights and sounds of his homeland via ink: his right leg is adorned with images of various iconic tourist attractions including a famous cable car, the Porto Torre dos Clérigos, and that beloved Portuguese instrument, a Fado guitar.

If ever Toby 'undercut' Alderweireld feels a pang of homesickness for Belgium, he has only to look at his right arm where lurks a detailed rendering of Antwerp Cathedral, minus the gift shop.

Arsenal midfielder Aaron Ramsey suffered to acquire these Welsh vistas: 'Most of these guys use that numbing cream, but being Welsh, I did not use any of that.'

'No one can take away your pain, so don't let anyone take away your happiness.' In 2012, not long after receiving a driving ban for doing 145mph on the A1, Arsenal left back André Santos commissioned Croatian artist Damir Stancic to install this elaborate, non-ironic, multi-font inscription on his left leg. The painstaking process was filmed and posted on YouTube.

Players derive comfort from heart-warming clichés

Too young to have developed a cynical attitude towards platitudes, players take them at face value and, in so doing, derive emotional comfort from them – which is what we were always supposed to do in the first place, so the laughs are on us cynics. For easy access – unless it's on your bum, in which case you will need a mirror or two – players archive these needlepoint-worthy declarations on their bodies.

Stoke City defender Glen Johnson's back declares that 'Everyman dies, but not every man lives', which is very twee, but also kind of makes sense. Making a great deal less sense, his right arm wistfully informs

us that 'Everything happens for a reason'. This is clearly, if I may say so, total bollocks. Every footballer's life – and every non-footballer's life – is a chaotic series of random contingencies, where *nothing* happens for a reason.

'Pain is temporary, victory is forever', scream Daniel Agger's ankles. In the coming years, as the retired Danish national and former Liverpool central defender ages and has to deal with joint pain or piles, one suspects that he and his ankles may well have a change of heart.

Players like to dream

The left hand of Marco Reus – attacking midfielder, winger or striker for Borussia Dortmund – is emblazoned with the stirring Oprah quote, 'The biggest adventure you can have is to live your dreams.' Sorry lads, but it is hard to think of anything more sick-making than living your dreams … like the one where you are locked in a Primark WC and told to eat your own hair by a disembodied voice, while clutching an aardvark. Players do not share my qualms about living one's dreams, however, as evidenced by the fact that Memphis Depay elected to emblazon his chest with the words 'dream chaser'. My definition of the word 'dreams' may well be too literal. For footballers, as for all sportsmen, 'dreams' are a polite euphemism for 'stop-at-nothing ambitions'.

On a sincerely dreamy note, Raheem Sterling's arm tattoo depicts a ten-year-old boy staring up in wonder at Wembley Stadium's famous arch, accompanied by the statement, 'It's a dream'. The Man City midfielder explains: 'Wembley was literally around the corner. I used to ride my bike round this little car park that was by the stadium. It's something that I've always wanted – to play for England and be the best I can be as a footballer.' Sweet.

Players like foreign languages

'*Veni, vidi, vici*' (I came, I saw, I conquered), declares Martin Skrtel's ribcage. Players love foreign languages, especially dead ones. Latin inscriptions such as '*Per ardua ad astra*' (through hardship to the stars) and '*Perfectio in Spiritu*' (perfection in the spirit – see Beckham's right arm) are popular with many lads. These ancient bursts of Latin wisdom add a whiff of Oxbridge gravitas to the 'brand' of any player.

A Sanskrit tattoo on Theo Walcott's right wrist translates as 'Beautiful, Blessed, Strong, Intelligent', dedicated respectively to his sister Hollie, his father Don, his brother Ashley and his mother Lynne (if I were Lynne I would have rather had 'beautiful' than 'intelligent', but let's not start a family row). Like yours truly, the Arsenal forward grew up in Berkshire, where Sanskrit, I can assure you, is the lingua franca.

The inside of Olivier Giroud's right arm declares, in olde worlde script, '*Dominus regit me et nihil mihi deerit*'. Translation: 'the Lord is my shepherd, I shall not want'. In an Arsenal-sponsored YouTube video, Giroud translates it as, 'God is my shepherd, and nothing will miss me'.

Regarding dodgy translations: players must be particularly vigilant about checking the current translation of these ancient tongues. Living languages can also present problems, as John Carew will attest. The former Aston Villa forward sports a neck tattoo that reads '*Ma Vie, Mes Régles*', the intended meaning of which is 'My life, my rules'. The error is on the word '*régles*', which with a correct è accent would mean 'rules'. Unfortunately for Mr Carew, his tattoo, with its incorrect é, could be misread as 'My life, my menstruation'.

'Life and death are determined by fate, rank and riches decreed by Heaven', declares Beckham's ribcage, in Chinese characters. A lovely graphic, beautifully placed, but again, is it really true? Were the Beckham rank and riches 'decreed by Heaven' or are they a function of sweat, drive, luck, creativity and strategy?

Players love Death

'Death', in the imagination of any footballer, can occur under a wide variety of circumstances: being axed, benched, bitten, nutted, hairdryered by your manager, receiving a driving ban after you just sprang for a new Lambo, being spanked by a lesser team in front of 80,000 howling fans, having your girlfriend nicked by a teammate, or getting sent off while your children – whose faces are tattooed on your extremities – watch from the stands. David Luiz would probably characterize the 2014 World Cup 7:1 denouement as a death experience.

Sheffield Wednesday striker Stephen Fletcher has a terrifying gothic-horror death-skull'n'roses tattooed on his leg, which is rad, but pales in comparison to the efforts of Daniel Agger. No other player has an entire Nordic graveyard rendered on his back. Graveyard-adjacent is the phrase '*Memento Mori*' (remember you shall die), along with '*Mors certa, hora incerta*' (Death is certain, the hour is uncertain).

Sometimes players use their tattoos to memorialize others – Jack Wilshere commemorates the death of an uncle in a car crash and Theo Walcott remembers a brother – but most 'death' tattoos are metaphorical or philosophical in nature. Neymar has, at the time of writing, two death-themed tattoos. '*Todo passa*' (everything passes) declares his elegant neck. As with so many footballer tattoos, the inscription is demonstrably untrue. Sorry, but everything does not pass. Horrible events, as footie players are painfully aware, have a way of lingering in the collective imagination and stinking up decades of one's life. But Neymar's left arm picks up the slack with a more realistic/nihilistic take on death: 'Life's a joke'. Says the man himself: 'I really identify with this tattoo. You can't take life too seriously. You have to enjoy every moment.'

Given the comet-like career span of the lads in question, it's not really surprising that they spend time watching the Grim Reaper in the rear-view mirror. Like ballet dancers and fashion models, footie players live with the sell-by date of Damocles hanging over their cockatiels. Ezequiel Lavezzi, the Argentine national and forward for Hebei China Fortune, sports a tattooed gun pointing down from his waistband, suggesting either a changing-room shoot-out, imminent self-castration, or both.

PSG central midfielder Marco Verratti sports a trippy fluorescent Mexican Day of the Dead skull on his left deltoid.

'Pistols at groin', declares Lavezzi's provocative tatt.

Daniel Agger, two-time Danish footballer of the year, is smothered in deadhead ink. He has already tee'd up his post-footie career by becoming a licensed tattoo artist.

'My new tattoo is Jesus being carried by three cherubs. Obviously the cherubs are my boys, so my thought of it is that at some point they are going to need to look after me and that's what they're doing in the picture. **It means a lot**.'

David Beckham in 2011

Players are in touch with their feelings

'You don't choose your family. They are God's gift to you, as you are to them', reads an inscription on the lower-left torso of Liverpool centre-back Dejan Lovren. In the middle of the last century the only member of the average working-class family who received these kinds of effusive declarations was the budgie. Sentimental family snaps were stashed in a chocolate box under the living-room couch. Excessive displays of affection were met with suspicion: clearly you had either been drinking or you were going a bit mental. Cut to 2017: feelings and emotions are lovingly inked onto footballer bodies, surrounded by cascading hearts and flowers.

Arsenal right back Mathieu Debuchy sports the names of his children Manon, Lukas and Lalou on his legs and the bottom of his back. He considers his left arm his best work of art: it's a summary of his family life, including his children's birthdays, his wedding, his wife's name and a rosary. Also check out Atlético Madrid striker Fernando Torres: Olalla (the missus) is memorialized on one forearm and Nora (the daughter) is on the other.

At the beginning of the 2016/17 season, Liverpool midfielder Philippe Coutinho explained how he spent his post-season holidays: 'I got some new tattoos, including one of my daughter … I had it done in Brazil. It hurt a lot – it took five hours to do and was done all in one go! … I don't have plans for any more now … only if I have another child.' What might be the reason for these touching displays of parental commitment? Are those laissez-faire, fag-smoking mums and dads of my youth simply a thing of the past? It is only natural that, in today's world of relentlessly conscientious parenting, a peripatetic jet-lagged footballer might feel he was short-changing his sprogs. His feelings of guilt

can be assuaged, masochistically and expensively, by tattooing beloved names, and faces, onto his body. He is also, on a purely pragmatic level, less likely to forget their birthdays if the dates are gouged into his skin.

The sharing of feelings has become the norm, even with super-macho footie players. In fact, these inked-up gladiators, like Sergio Ramos, are out front leading the sentimental charge.

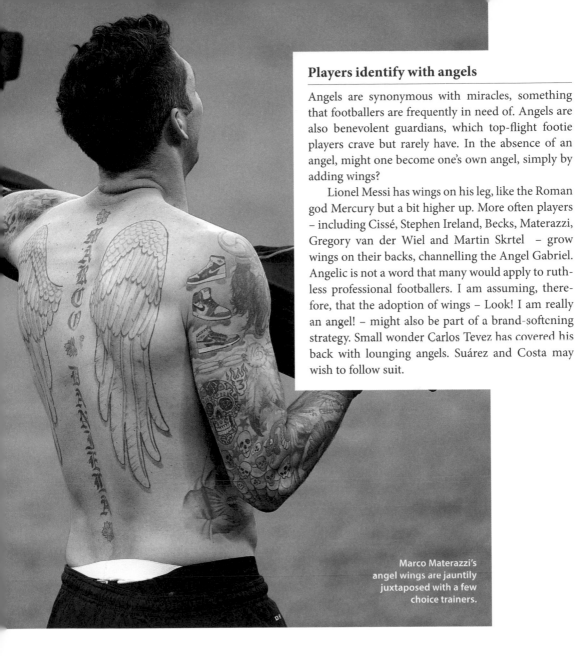

Players identify with angels

Angels are synonymous with miracles, something that footballers are frequently in need of. Angels are also benevolent guardians, which top-flight footie players crave but rarely have. In the absence of an angel, might one become one's own angel, simply by adding wings?

Lionel Messi has wings on his leg, like the Roman god Mercury but a bit higher up. More often players – including Cissé, Stephen Ireland, Becks, Materazzi, Gregory van der Wiel and Martin Skrtel – grow wings on their backs, channelling the Angel Gabriel. Angelic is not a word that many would apply to ruthless professional footballers. I am assuming, therefore, that the adoption of wings – Look! I am really an angel! – might also be part of a brand-softening strategy. Small wonder Carlos Tevez has covered his back with lounging angels. Suárez and Costa may wish to follow suit.

Marco Materazzi's angel wings are jauntily juxtaposed with a few choice trainers.

Players are impulsive

The most impulsive thing a player can do is to get inked up with the logo of his current club. Lukas Podolski's old Cologne club tattoo did not go unnoticed on the Arsenal pitch where he later played.

Though wisely reticent to tattoo their current club logo, players frequently memorialize other equally ephemeral aspects of their lives, most notably their WAGs. Many players impulsively adorn their bodies with depictions of the mother of their children, only to divorce her shortly thereafter. In a true fingers-crossed moment, American star Landon Donovan and his first wife, actress Bianca Kajlich, acquired matching hummingbird tattoos because 'hummingbirds mate for life'. Sadly they divorced in 2010. Meanwhile, on 8 February 2013 the *Daily Mail* revealed that Leicester City's Danny Simpson had stepped up his romance with pop singer Tulisa by getting his'n'hers tattoos. Alas, by 25 May that same year the paper reported the romance was 'All Over'.

Above Man U's Zlatan Ibrahimović and Man City's Aleksandar Kolarov are both koi devotees, which sets the stage for a rainy, fishy, Northern derby. (Many of Zlat's tatts evaporated from subsequent photographs, sparking rumours that Mr Ibrahimović had embarked on a major regime of laser removal. It then emerged that many of the original tattoos in this photo were temporary and had washed off.)

Left Raul Meireles and wife Ivone giving their ink a good dunking.

Players like koi and dragons

Koi fish and dragons, standard motifs in yakuza tattoos, are drenched in the kind of symbolism that appeals to footballers. It's all about swimming against the tide, often scaling a waterfall and reaching the dragon's gate, at which point – natch – you, the koi, turn into a dragon.

PINKY BOOTS

'YOU'VE BEEN SHITE, SON, IN YOUR DAFT PINK BOOTS.'

Players have no say in their kit, with the exception of their footwear, and with their footwear it's gone from having a say to having a primal screech. I refer to the wearing of those shrill fluorescent boots.

The macho ethos of football started at the feet, down in the muck. In 1878 the lads of Newton Heath, eventually to become Manchester United, played footie in their work clogs. This is back when men were men, and the stench of foot odour mixed with carbolic was their only fragrance.

Men continued to be men well into the twentieth century. The epicentre of manliness at any club was definitely the boot room. In the last century, Liverpool's legendary boot room – Barney Ronay describes it as 'a dark, sweaty, sock-stinking place' – was the sacrosanct retreat where the strategic powwows took place that propelled Liverpool to win the First Division title 13 times.

Cut to the dawn of the pink boot. It is hard to imagine what managers like Bill Shankly or Bob Paisley would have made of today's shocking-pink Barbie boots. My reservations about the fluorescent boot trend are ultimately more nannying than judgmental. I applaud the gender-bending audacity. My concerns are 100 per cent practical. When boots were poo-brown and functional, covered in mud, they were at least camouflaged. If you wanted to stomp on an opponent you had to make a real effort to find his boot.

> 'Back in my time, and I sound old now, it was black and white boots and that was it. Now you've got snoods, people wearing headphones when they're doing interviews, which I find disrespectful, pink boots, green boots.'
>
> Notts County manager and former England captain, Paul Ince, reminiscing in 2011

> 'I've wanted to play in pink boots since I was little. The only way anyone can top me now is to wear diamond-encrusted boots.'
>
> Arsenal and Denmark striker Nicklas Bendtner (pictured) in 2008

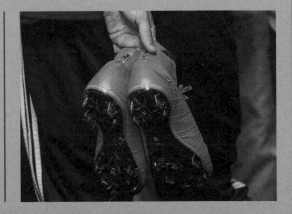

NO ACCESSORIZING
ON THE PITCH

'I'm not a tights wearer. Maybe in my own household, but not on the pitch.'

Real Madrid team-member Michael Owen, declining an opportunity to combat arctic temperatures in Kiev in 2014

'MY MUM WOULD KILL ME IF I WORE GLOVES IN A GAME.'

West Ham and England winger Matt Jarvis in 2013

'A big difference [between English and French football] is the underwear players have. Pink, orange, green, fluorescent - and they play wearing that, too.'

England midfielder Joe Cole, after joining Lille in 2011

Costa and Azpilicueta. Why so many masks at Chelsea? Is this yet another example of that legendary King's Road preening?

'I HOPE PUMA DOES NOT MAKE CONDOMS.'

Xherdan Shaqiri after four Swiss shirts rip easily in the 2016 Euros draw with France

Gaudy ink and psycho barnets are a common sight on pitches across the globe. Fashion accessories? Not so much. Before every game, players ceremoniously strip off their Bulgari chains, Tag Heuer watches, Cartier bangles, diamond-stud earrings, nipple-piercings and any other man-jazzles with laceration potential. Safety concerns dictate that players face the lumpen masses, and each other, sans adornment. Courageously, they take to the field accessory-free, knowing that a blood-soaked bandage is about as good as it's ever going to get. Unless, of course, the lad in question is lucky enough to break his nose.

Any player who breaks his nose and elects *not* to wear one of those fabulous Zorro masks is probably suffering from a very dire concussion indeed. What else could explain the failure to recognize such a magnificent accessory-portunity. Those sinister black masks are not only stylish, they are historically stylish, evoking as they do the glamour of ancient Greek armoured helmets.

Examples of mask-wearers are in no short supply, but standouts are Fernando Torres when he was at Chelsea, Cesc Fàbregas, also at Chelsea, and César Azpilicueta, aka 'Dave', of Chelsea. John Terry, also of Chelsea, even wore an avant-garde transparent jelly version. Conclusion: Chelsea loves a fashion accessory.

Players like to big up themselves

Nocerino is running round the pitch with 'NOCERINO 23' emblazoned on his tramp-stamp zone, despite now being over 30 and wearing the #22 shirt for Orlando City. 'King Arthur' screeches the left bicep of Chilean mohawk devotee Arturo Vidal. Many players elect to adorn themselves with their own names, including Southend United's Nile Ranger and Argentinian Andrés D'Alessandro, who even added his own face. This frantic self-labelling will come in handy towards the end of their lives, especially if they are unfortunate enough to lose their marbles. Extra handy for carers – 'Morning Mister … er … Ranger! How are we feeling today?'

Mario Balotelli somehow resisted the temptation to tattoo himself with his own name, opting instead for the next best thing, a first-person singular Genghis Khan quote on his chest that reads: 'If you had not committed great sins/God would not have sent/ A punishment like me upon you'. The award for the greatest self-glorifying tattoo of all time, though, surely goes to Leroy Sané. In 2017 the Man City winger smothered his entire back with a sweeping, billboard-sized depiction of, yes, Leroy Sané, celebrating a Champions League goal against Monaco. Many questioned the hubristic nature of Sané's ink, especially given the fact that City were subsequently beaten by Monaco on away goals, dropping out of the competition before the quarter final. However, the tattoo gods chose not to punish Sané: at the time of writing he has scored six goals in six Premier League appearances in the 2017/18 season.

Handy for identification purposes if you are washed up on a beach.

Players are in denial

Ibrahimović, Ozil and Cissé have something unusual in common – they each sport a tattoo which reads 'Only God can judge me'. This is a nice idea but, once again, clearly untrue. People – refs, pundits, managers, players, fans, his cleaning lady – are judging Zlatan Ibrahimović morning, noon and night. Arsène Wenger's beady judgmental eyes are boring into Ozil's back every time he gets the ball. A retired Psychedelic Ninja like Cissé has been judged for his plays, to mention nothing of his personal style, for his entire life. No amount of ink can stop this global, 24-hour judge-athon.

Players are prone to magical thinking

The unrelenting pressure to win produces an almost woo-woo culture of primitive ritual and superstition. Kevin-Prince Boateng, for example, commissioned a spider web tattoo on an injury-prone knee, because spider webs 'always come back'.

Players love fashion
(but recognize that it changes)

Welshman Robbie Savage, provocative pundit and former player, once commissioned a tattoo of the Armani logo on his arm … then had it removed.

Players can occasionally get political

Maradona commemorates Che Guevara and Fidel Castro, the latter in gratitude for having facilitated his cure for cocaine addiction, while Sergio Ramos commemorates two terrorist attacks, 9/11 and Madrid 11-M – one on each bicep.

Che, Maradona, Fidel and a couple of lucky Cohibas.

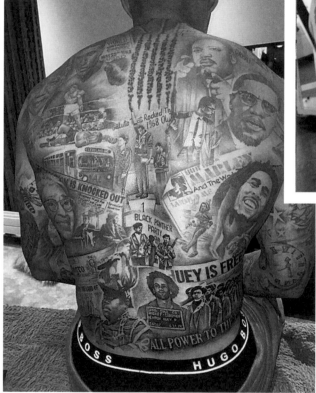

At the beginning of the 2017/18 season Watford's Andre Gray unveiled what can only be described as a mural, memorializing the American Civil Rights struggle. Andre endured nine eight-hour sessions in the chair, presumably lying on his face. Who says young people don't care about history?

Players sometimes suffer from OCD

Many player tattoos are ill-considered and randomly placed, to the point of madness. By contrast, Colorado Rapids goalie and former Everton star Tim Howard displays tattoos that appear painstakingly laid out. In Howard's case, one suspects the highly considered approach is more a function of his obsessive-compulsive tendencies. The beloved goalie has been very forthcoming about his lifelong struggle with Tourette's syndrome. On an even more obsessive note, Dutch professional Nigel de Jong appears to be, slowly but surely, covering his entire body with meticulously placed tribal ornamentations. As a result, Nige gets my award for the *least* random tattoos in football.

Nigel de Jong's body art is like an exquisite burgeoning doily which, one assumes, will eventually cover his entire body.

Tim Howard is a meticulous
art director, trapped in the
body of a goalie.

Players are matey with their tattoo providers

Arsenal right back Mathieu Debuchy's best pal is a tattoo artist named Gégé. Many of Gégé's waking hours have been devoted to memorializing the Debuchy clan on the Debuchy body. Roberto Lopez, Messi's tattoo artist and a guest at his wedding, is so committed to his favourite client that he has publicly vowed – via a sign installed in the window of his Barcelona parlour – to inflict additional agony on any client who dares to talk smack about his Lionel. Meanwhile, the lads all speak highly of Louis Molloy. Beckham, who, it must be acknowledged, was way out front with the tattoo trend, calls Mr Molloy 'my Guardian Angel'. Though retired, Beckham remains a significant influence on the style choices of young players, particularly with regard to tattoos.

Piotrek Taton earned the undying respect of Carlos Tevez when he covered his back in those mysterious angel figures. 'Thanks, friend, for your magnificent art!!!', trilled the Argentine legend, adding, 'You're the greatest.'

In conclusion, tattoos not only relieve players' stress but they also, like bonkers barnets, provide the lads with an outlet for personal expression. In an era when players are encouraged to be mute and non-controversial, tattoos offer a way to be heard, an explosive, indelible medium of communication over which managers and club owners have no control. We fans are the lucky beneficiaries.

But there's more: footie is turning into Formula One. In the last few years every visual aspect of the football-going experience has become smothered in corporate logos: the stadiums, the shirts, the TV graphics, even the step-and-repeat backdrops of the pre/post-match interviews, are all awash with branding visuals. If you had told players like Ricardo Zamora or Stanley Matthews that in the future players would be dribbling away with strange words like Aon, Bimbo, Plastic Box Shop, Etihad, Dafabet and Lubrax slapped across their chests they would never have believed you. In a commendable challenge to this blizzard of corporate logos, the players now tattoo their bodies with mysterious artworks and verbiage that express non-corporate, highly idiosyncratic thoughts and impulses, both deep and shallow.

Macho macho men: Neymar and Alves discarding
their corporate logos and sponsorship graphics,
and unleashing their tattooed machismo.

Tattoos arc also a way to push back against the trolls and haters.
Players attempt to immunize themselves against corrosive, emascu-
lating, diminishing social media takedowns by expressing simple
old-fashioned bravado, positivity and optimism. Pride and Glory!
Tattoos are a reminder to players to amp up the virility and bravery –
in other words, *to butch it up a bit*. In an era of soundproofed wellness
rooms, private planes, millionaire pay cheques, gluten-free cuisine,
perfect bods and hyper-fitness, tattoos help maintain notions of fear-
lessness and ferocity: as the Caligula quote on Beckham's crowded
left arm says, 'Let them hate as long as they fear.'

There is one notable hold-out to the ink culture in football:
Cristiano Ronaldo, who claims that he has eschewed tattoos in
order to be able to give blood (the NHS recommends a four-month
lag time between giving blood and getting tattooed or pierced). I
suspect that if he wanted a tattoo he would get one. Which leads me
to believe that he has simply opted out. Or maybe he is scared of
needles. Or maybe he has seized upon the concept of non-tattooing
as yet another way to float above the rest of y'all.

'Cristiano strolls the meandering driveway down
to the sand-coloured boxes of his eight-car garage,
where he keeps some (but not all) of his fleet,
including (reportedly) a Maserati GranCabrio,
Bentley Continental GT, Porsche Cayenne Turbo,
Lamborghini Aventador, Ferrari 599 GTO, Rolls-Royce
Phantom, Aston Martin DB9, team-issue Audi, etc.'
GQ USA, February 2016

'Why shouldn't I drive a Ferrari? It's not like I'm buying drugs or something. And anyway Beckham has six of them!'

Former Ajax striker Mido

5. Car Porn

The Boys and Their Million-Dollar Toys

Of all the luxurious indulgences that a successful footballer might award himself – booze, bets or Balmain – a conspicuously glamorous, ridiculously low-to-the-ground, phallically symbolic motor is the one that really seems to hit the spot.

While Hollywood flagellates itself with climate-change concerns and talk of carbon footprints, Footie World is turbo-charging its brains out with fleets of glinting supercars. William Gallas has a Chrome Mercedes McLaren. Benzema and Ronaldo both drive Bugatti Veyrons, which, when I last checked, were priced at $2.5 million. Del Piero has a Lancia Delta. John Terry drives a 1964 SLR Ferrari. Raheem Sterling is poised to buy a BMW i8. His fleet of six comprises a matte black Range Rover Evoque, an Audi S7 Sportback, an Audi Q7, a Mercedes-AMG C63, a Smart Fortwo and a Range Rover Sport. Why the BMW? He needs a different car for each day of the week.

Above Man U winger Jesse Lingard getting a tad upstaged by his murdered-out Batmobile of a Range Rover.

Right And this is just his fiancée's car! While she drives this £235,000 Bentley GTC, Stephen Ireland, the Stoke City midfielder, drives a customized Audi R8 with Barbie-pink rims and matching grill.

Footie players have become synonymous with swanky motors. When they deviate from the script the effect can be jarring. In 2017 Wayne Rooney blasted into the headlines again when he was busted for drink-driving. While Coleen was holidaying with their fourth child on board, Wayne was overcoming his shyness in an Alderley Edge hotspot named The Bubble Room. He made the fateful decision to ferry home a new acquaintance in her own vehicle. Regular footie watchers all had the same reaction: Wayne Rooney driving a VW Bug? No wonder he got pulled over.

Above Retired winger El Hadji Diouf arriving at, or possibly leaving, Rio Ferdinand's Rosso restaurant in Manchester, in his McLaren SLR supercar.

Right Pierre-Emerick Aubameyang – who plays for Borussia Dortmund and captains the Gabon national team – blinding people on the streets of Milan with his golden Porsche in 2016.

Below While Man City's Kevin De Bruyne swipes left, occasional teammate Samir Nasri prepares to slither into his $200,000 Lamborghini.

Since this picture was taken, Real Madrid's Gareth Bale has, allegedly, begun to rethink his addiction to supercars. He is convinced that driving Lambos and Ferraris has contributed to his hamstring injuries.

Top Arsenal attacking midfielder and car-oholic Mesut Ozil in his Mercedes G-Wagen.

Above Celtic winger Scott Sinclair is giving us the Hired Assassin look. When your Ferrari is worth over $200,000, it's good to adopt an intimidating appearance.

Footballers, in other words, are barking batshit mental for cars. And why not? What, pray, is the point of being a cash-rich professional footballer if you can't screech into the training car park on a set of hot rims. Players like Emmanuel Adebayor, Mesut Ozil, Karim Benzema and Pierre-Emerick Aubameyang own massive multi-million-dollar car collections, which easily rival that of Ronaldo and make me very glad I am not responsible for checking the fluids and general Simonizing.

CAR TROUBLE

'My new yellow Ferrari broke down on the M42. I ended up on the side of the motorway with everyone driving past giving me "V" and "wanker" signs, even old men and women.'

Player turned pundit Robbie Savage in 2009

Extreme youth + extreme wealth + extreme automobiles: it's a volatile mix. Borussia Dortmund striker Marco Reus drove around in his Aston Martin for three years without a driver's licence. Ahmed Hossam Hussein Abdelhamid, the former Ajax striker known as Mido, had an airport freak-out when, allegedly, he returned from a trip to Egypt to discover that his car was *not* parked exactly where he left it, directly in front of the departure lounge at Schiphol airport.

'Double parking - one of [Balotelli's] favourite pastimes - results in a mountain of parking tickets. In Manchester, over the course of twelve months, he collects traffic fines amounting to over thirteen thousand dollars.'

Maarten Bax recapping Mario Balotelli's civic pride in *Sex, Drugs and Soccer*

Car Porn: the early years. In August 1938 Bryn Jones transferred from Wolves to Arsenal for a world record fee of £14,000, triggering outraged debate in the House of Commons.

The Sixties

Pre-war, car ownership was unusual. Most lads were cycling to training or taking public transport. The car/footie symbiosis did not gather momentum until the 1960s, jump-started by the 1961 maximum wage abolition. Suddenly players could afford to indulge in the middle-class delights of car ownership.

Hugh Hefner's *Playboy* magazine ethos combined with the Bond movies that dominated culture at the time to offer a swanky new definition of masculinity. In place of the 1950s 'angry young men' with their bicycles, stained ties and endless introspection, we were now force-fed images of Technicolor hedonists from across the pond, like Elvis in his gigantic Cadillacs and James Dean in his killer Porsche.

How did he decide between leopard, zebra, ocelot or tiger?
Rangers legend Jim Baxter (seen here c. 1962) was a tough, heroic Scotsman with, apparently, a rather camp side.

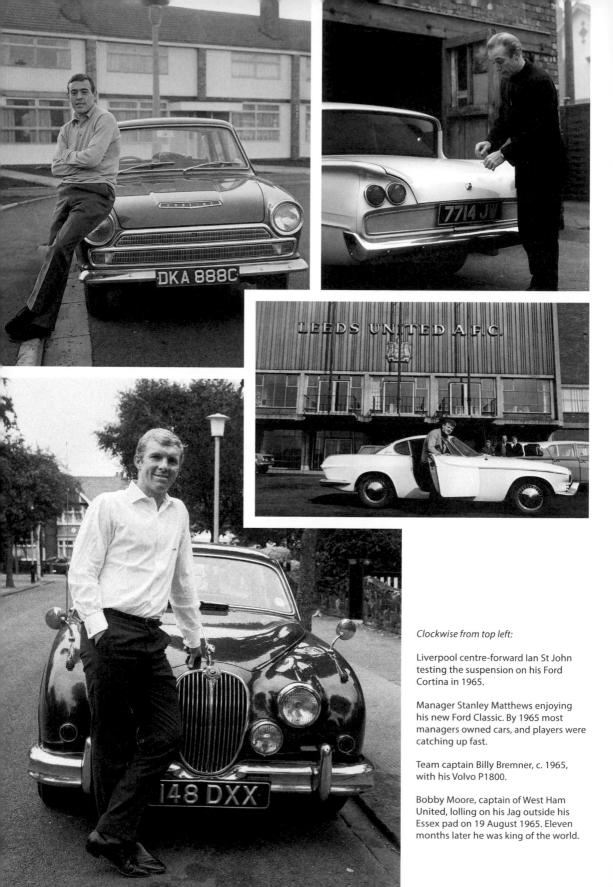

Clockwise from top left:

Liverpool centre-forward Ian St John testing the suspension on his Ford Cortina in 1965.

Manager Stanley Matthews enjoying his new Ford Classic. By 1965 most managers owned cars, and players were catching up fast.

Team captain Billy Bremner, c. 1965, with his Volvo P1800.

Bobby Moore, captain of West Ham United, lolling on his Jag outside his Essex pad on 19 August 1965. Eleven months later he was king of the world.

'I used to go missing a lot …
Miss Canada, Miss United
Kingdom, Miss World.'

George Best in 1966, pictured here indulging in a little interpretive dancing,
with his Jag and with Miss UK Jennifer Lowe

Male status was now defined by money, gorgeous girlfriends
and motors. Racing superstars like Stirling Moss were envied and
idolized. Yes, a number of middle-class kids trudged to Woodstock
seeking spiritual enlightenment in Nature, but not the working class,
and certainly not the footballers. They set their sights on Brands
Hatch, Goodwood or Le Mans.

The Sixties saw an explosion in consumption as personal expression. For footballers, cars were every bit as important as those
Carnaby Street schmattas. The lads quickly discovered that no other
purchase could fire up their machismo quite like a phallic, ferocious,
chick-magnetizing, spiffy ride. Footballers may have lacked the
Euro-sophistication of international playboys, but they nonetheless
aspired to the same fast groovy lifestyle, albeit in Grimsby or Brum,
paving the way for today's car-oholics.

Man City legend Mike Summerbee driving his
Volvo P1800 – the model driven by Roger Moore
in *The Saint* – popping 'Ruby Tuesday' into the
sound system, c. 1967.

The Seventies

The 1970s saw an explosion of car consumption and flamboyant design. The era is characterized by daring colours and a brutalist aesthetic. For top players, multiple autos were becoming the norm. George Best drove a Rolls-Royce Silver Ghost, a Lotus Europa, a Merc WII2 and sundry E-Types. Not content with just having a Tannenbaum-green Ferrari (the German press dubbed him 'the Porsche-driving socialist'), Günter Netzer also owned a retina-searing tangerine Ferrari Daytona.

In Hunter Davies's book *The Glory Game* he documents a year in the life of the 1972 Tottenham Hotspur squad which, at the time, included captain Mullery, Jennings, Peters, Chivers and Perryman. Lurking among the wealth of data in this trusty book is an inventory of the cars – a tantalizing and diverse selection of Jags, Rovers, Capris and sports cars – that were owned by the players. We are still decades away from today's multi-million-dollar supercar collections, but the selection is louche and lively.

Johan Cruyff dressed very 'Shaft', warming his zitvlak on his Citroën SM Maserati in 1973.

Clockwise from above:

Eusébio and his wife Flora enjoying a three-way with their Saab Sonett III in 1972.

Former World Cup gladiators Geoff Hurst and Bobby Moore picking up their freebie Cortinas from Ford in Brentwood in 1970. The Cortina was to become the best-selling car of the decade. As per usual, Bobby is relentlessly promoting a trench from his own line of suede and leather jackets and coats.

1972. Franz 'Kaiser' Beckenbauer resting the spout of his teapot on the front of his BMW Automatic.

Above George Best, the retailer, and his MGB GT, c. 1970.

Left Wolves royalty David Wagstaffe, his Jag and his WAG Barbara, sporting a magnificent teased bouffant.

Frank Worthington and his girlfriend Vicki. Back in the early 1970s a girl could put fingermarks on the Lotus without being admonished. It was a less prissy time.

The relationship between footie, hedonism and cars exploded in this decade. Frank Worthington, who spent these years playing at Huddersfield, Leicester and Bolton, did more than most to unite this holy trinity. When Worthington wanted to nip from the Twisted Wheel or Slack Alice in Manchester to the Tahiti Two in Huddersfield or the Gatto Bianco in Bradford, only an MGB or Lotus would do the trick. His passion for cars is vividly recollected in his bawdy, thigh-slapping memoir, *One Hump or Two: The Frank Worthington Story*: 'In my time I've had all manner from beaten up VWs and Saabs, to MGBs, a Mustang, the latest model Vauxhalls, Fords and BMWs – I even had a Lada once.'

The players of Frank's era started the now time-honoured tradition of attempting suicide on the way to the training ground. According to Worthington, 'every day was race day, with all the lads vying to get back from training first. There was Les Chapman in his green TR5, myself in my MGB, Dick Krzywicki in what he referred to as his 'shree'-litre Capri and Jimmy McGill in the maroon Cortina with the klaxon you could hear all over town.'

Arsenal legend Charlie George + regrettable perm + regret-free Rolls-Royce, c. 1975.

Accidents were inevitable, careers cut short. Worthington's Huddersfield Town teammate Billy Legg fell asleep at the wheel of his maroon Cortina and smashed into a roundabout, sustaining a crushed windpipe. Recalls Frank, 'Billy owes his life to the quick thinking of a policeman who performed a tracheotomy with a Biro'. Frank was luckier. He fell asleep at the wheel of a Buick Riviera, bounced off the central reservation but survived to tell the tale. No Biro needed.

When Frank's career starts going south, the decline is poignantly reflected in his ride, 'a second-hand Mini with blood on the seat', and later still, 'an old beaten up left-hand-drive Saab which I'd bought for ninety-eight pounds at the Measham car auctions, complete with Jesus sticker on the back window'.

The Eighties and Nineties

The Gazza/Merson years arrived. Players would meet at a pub, get plastered and dare each other to eat the contents of the nearest ashtray. The wheels began coming off.

Arsenal megastar Tony Adams was a car freak who lived for his Clarion sound system, amplifier and Pioneer speakers. Having a car was more than just an efficient way to get to training. It was his ticket to the high life, by which I mean nipping back and forward between Ra Ra's in Islington, The Albion in Rainham and Hollywood's in Romford. 'My profession was also emblazoned on my car: "Footballers make the best lovers" said a tongue-in-cheek sticker on my Mark IV Ford Cortina which I loved to bits with its Grand Prix S-tyres and tiny steering wheel', recalls Adams in his touching memoir, *Addicted*. Mr Adams's chronicle of misdeeds included smashing glasses over his own head, claiming to be injured but then going dancing at Tramp, falling asleep while minding the baby, thereby giving said baby the opportunity to eat a lipstick, and that legendary smash-up that landed him in the clink.

In 1982 this BMW cost Newcastle FC £20,000, and Kevin Keegan was allowed to keep it as long as he remained at the club. KK scored 48 goals in 78 appearances for the Magpies.

Above Laurie Cunningham in 1982, larging it with a Porsche in Madrid, where, seven years after this photo was taken, he died in a car crash, aged 33.

Left Gary Lineker manspreading on his Toyota, during his mid-'80s Everton moment. Not only did Lineker score ten goals for England in FIFA World Cup finals, he also got better looking and more stylish as he got older.

Above Ryan Giggs – the Man U lifer went on to become the most decorated footballer in history – saw fit to wear a shellsuit to accept his freebie Ford Escort, a birthday gift, c. 1991.

Right Mr and Mrs Beckham in 1998, giving the distinct impression that they are attempting to nick their own Porsche.

By the late 1990s, footie began to sober up: in 1997, *The Glory Game* is reprinted, complete with an updated car line-up. This is the Spurs of Sheringham, Wilson, Howells and Rosenthal. The hedonism is waning and the supercar madness of the twenty-first century has yet to arrive. Filling the void is a strangely posh, homogenous and thoroughly respectable car line-up that includes five Mercedes and four BMWs. A new grown-up, and mostly German, aesthetic has arrived. Safety and function prevail: *#nannystate*.

Mr Beckham gassing up the Ferrari in Alderley Edge in 2002.

Goodbye rusty Cortinas, hello gleaming Lambos

When Bruce Rioch was the manager of Bolton Wanderers back in the early '90s, he was proud of the fact that the entire squad showed up at training packed into four cars. All the lads lived in the same estate. There is something distinctly appealing about the simplicity of this concept: one team, one housing estate, four cars. Today's players, by contrast, seem a tad encumbered. They often appear a little anxious around their gleaming 'investment' vehicles. Are they simply too wealthy, and too prestige-obsessed, to enjoy the cheap thrill of a bouncing Cortina with a tacky bumper sticker?

The late writer A.A. Gill once identified a contemporary phenomenon that afflicts super-rich people, which he called Perfection Anxiety: 'Only the fathomlessly rich suffer from Perfection Anxiety. There is no relativity to wealth. It's all absolutes. It's either impeccable, the best, the rarest, or it might as well be Walmart.' Today's footballing car connoisseurs are poster children for this perfection anxiety. Wafting through their mini auto museums – whether the cars are rented, leased or purchased, their attitude is the same – they seem afflicted not just with a terror of scratches and stains, but also with a fear of missing out on something better. As Gill continued, 'New purchases become just a matter of upgrading. And this is where the Perfection Anxiety kicks in. What you need is to have not just the most but the very, very best.' I think it might be time for a second-hand Mini with dried blood on the seats. And don't forget your Biro.

Whether glam or blood-stained, the cars that Frank – and Tony and Gazza and Georgie – drove never upstaged their owners. They wore their various vehicles like a much-loved outfit. Their passion for autos seems earthy and virile. You can smell the Brut, the fags, the leather upholstery and the sweat.

There is hope: today's footie carscape is not entirely filled with precious million-dollar car collections. Every so often one encounters a player who is bucking the car porn trend. Freddie Ljungberg freaked out his teammates by riding his grandma's bicycle to training. And then there is Jan Vertonghen: while his teammates are gunning it in their Ferraris and Range Rovers, the Spurs defender drives a Ford Mustang GT. When training in Belgium he drives a Toyota Corolla, or rather his mother does – she likes to drop him off at training. Ma Vertonghen and Jan have lavished time and money on maintaining the family Corolla: this treasured vehicle was bought for his father, now deceased, and has great sentimental value.

When the weather turned chilly, both skins and suedes would break out a zipped Baracuta jacket known as a 'Harrington'.

'Now that we don't have war, what's wrong with a good punch-up? We're a nation of yobs. Without that characteristic, how did we colonize the world? With so many milksops, left-wing liberals and wetties around, I rejoice that some people keep up our historic spirit.'

The Dowager Marchioness of Reading, aged 79, on the hooliganism of England fans

6. Fans

The Mod, the Mad and the Malevolent

June 1968: Bobby Kennedy is assassinated. Gary Puckett & The Union Gap sing 'Lady Willpower'. Alan Mullery kicks Dobrivoje Trivić in the knackers, thereby becoming the first England player to be given a red card.

It happened during the European Championship semi-final against Yugoslavia. 'He raked his studs, whatever they were made of, down my calf. Blood started pouring out, and I just turned around and kicked him in the how's your fathers', recalled a misty Mullery, reminiscing about the incident in later years.

I remember 1968 quite vividly. A schoolmate and best pal named Jim Nutley scored a Saturday job selling clobber in a men's boutique near the Reading town centre. This establishment, suavely named Harvey Michael, serviced the needs of the hardest, meanest, football-lovin' skinheads in Reading. Overnight I found myself sitting in the front row of the most violent fashion show on Earth.

Come Saturday, I would stop by Harvey Michael and gossip with Jim. Every so often a customer, either a skinhead or the slightly less antisocial derivative, a suedehead, would wander in and Jim would go into his are-you-being-served mode. Whether suede or skin, the Harvey Michael clients were uniformly terrifying. Piss them off and they might come back and egg the place. (This actually happened. Jim spent days afterwards clawing congealing ovums from the fibres of various garments and placing them back into stock.)

As horrible as the mores were, I found myself drawn to the obsessive uniformity of the skin/suede hooligan style. As with the earlier mods, the skins and suedes had a demented preoccupation with rules and neatness. Like many fascistic styles, the look was strangely intoxicating.

The Reading footie skinheads took great pride in keeping their cherry red Doc Martens ridiculously well polished. They chose steel toecaps, a working man's protection, but equally well suited for 'putting the boot in' upon encountering rival fans. They wore tight calf-length Levi's 501s with turn-ups to show off their boots.

Skinheads wore button-down collared checked shirts – either Ben Sherman or the slightly cheaper brand Brutus – and favoured short sleeves. These preppy details were a nod to the mod roots of skinhead fashion. Red clip-on braces (suspenders) yanked the jeans upwards, creating many a moose-knuckle. Black pork pie hats, a Caribbean influence, were worn on the back of the head.

The skinheads overlapped majorly with the suedeheads. The differences were nuanced. Basically suedeheads, with their slightly longer hair, appeared marginally less terrifying. Overall, suedeheads went for a more formal look, often completing their ensembles with navy or black Crombie overcoats, or single-vent jackets, in maroon or camel, sometimes worn over a wool slip-over (sleeveless pullover). Ties, tiepins and pocket hankies were common. In lieu of moose-knuckle Levi's, suedes wore Sta-Prest trousers in black, khaki or greyish-beige. Because of their more *soigné* appearance, suedeheads could hang out at pubs like The Peacock and larger venues like the Top Rank Ballroom, whereas the overtly antisocial skinheads were not welcome anywhere, except football matches, and 'welcome' is hardly the *mot juste*.

Instead of DMs, suedeheads favoured heavy black brogues called Royals, and the more sought-after Bass Weejuns, a quality tasselled loafer in black or oxblood. The latter were more acceptable to pub and club proprietors and almost certainly more likely to get you a decent 'salt', aka a bit of crumpet. On special occasions,

Tressy but tough. The early 1970s marked the beginning of the era when hooligans organized themselves into 'firms', like United's Red Army and City's Blazing Squad. For the next decade anyone going to a match might run foul of the Millwall Bushwackers, the Yid Army, the Naughty Forty, the Gremlins or the Suicide Squad.

SIR PAUL SMITH observes:

'These kids came from chaotic post-war backgrounds where parents wore whatever they could get their hands on. The new generation reacted to the shabbiness and randomness, so everything they wore became very, very considered. Mods, skinheads, smooths, casuals, all of that. It is so specific, and it keeps coming back. It is always going to be an influence on fashion.'

suedes, and occasionally skins, would break out a two-tone suit. Tailored from Trevira two-tone fabric, also confusingly known as 'Tonic', these suits had two popular colourways: blue/magenta or blue/green. These narrow, shiny, sharp suits have become, over the decades, a menswear icon that has inspired every designer from Paul Smith to Prada. When adopted by groups like The Specials and Madness, these two-tone whistles enjoyed a vigorous and well-deserved revival in the early 1980s. Companies like Merc and Jump the Gun keep the flame alive today. Who doesn't love a shiny suit, a black pork pie hat and a skinny tie? Female footie fans copied this look, compensating for the Rosa Klebb butchness of the attire by wearing astounding amounts of eye make-up. Their hair was worn in the short-on-the-top, long-at-the-sides style associated with pop goddess Julie Driscoll and Jane Fonda's character in the movie *Klute*.

The racism that was specifically linked to skinheads in the 1980s was not front and centre back then. There was, if anything, an unquestioning worship of West Indian culture. Reggae and ska were everything. Skinheads and suedes danced to The Upsetters' 'Return of Django', 'Long Shot Kick de Bucket' by the Pioneers, and of course – I vividly remember the day Jim scored a copy of this horny outlawed waxing – 'Wet Dream' by Max Romeo. Black dudes were referred to as 'spades', but in a reverential way. Suedeheads tended to be older and smoother and more into R&B or soul than reggae. Nevertheless, for both suedes and skins, black music was the only music that mattered.

Smooth Salford girls heading to Old Trafford in 1972.

Goodbye skins, hello smooths

In 1970 I left Reading behind and went to Manchester University. I travelled on the train with a schoolmate named Terry, a self-described 'greebo', who had long hair and wore leather jackets and faded jeans. We were excited about moving to 'the London of the North'. 'Let's go and see George Best play', said Terry. I was flabbergasted at the suggestion. Not because George was past his prime – it was, instead, the very real fear of being dismembered.

As scary as the Reading fans were, the Manchester skins were a hundred times more fearsome. Stylewise, I was moving into my Kensington Market glamrock period and Terry was a tall blond greaser. Waltzing onto the Stretford End together would have created a tribal collision, the equivalent of walking into oncoming traffic.

This situation did not prevent me from keeping a close eye on what the supporters were wearing. The best place to study footie-fan fashion was the Manchester town centre. All you had to do was hang out at Ivor's. This retail institution was the brainchild of an entrepreneurial bloke named Ivor Hazan. When George Best opened his clothing shop a few years prior, he had made a gentleman's agreement with Mr Hazan: I won't sell jeans and you won't sell suits. Ivor got the better half of the deal. The fans flocked and Ivor went on to open over 40 branches.

On Fridays and Saturdays the city centre was crawling with skins and suedeheads wearing footie scarves and carrying the distinctive and cheeky Ivor's shopping bags, citrus yellow with the words 'Stolen from Ivor's' slammed across both sides in black blocky letters. There were always a few extra coppers lurking outside Ivor's, just in case any groups of City and United fans encountered each other. Mostly things were peaceful. Entire hooligan families – mum, dad and kids, all dressed in Ben Sherman and Sta-Prest – would pour out onto the street, happily clutching their yellow 'Stolen from Ivor's' bags.

During the time I lived in Manchester, the fan style evolved dramatically. The rigid, brutal skinhead look was becoming an anachronism. The football supporters' hair was getting longer, and jeans and trousers were getting wider and wider. Suddenly, the hardest footie fans in England were wearing what amounted to palazzo pants with turn-ups. These were known as '22-inch parallels' and were available in denim and gabardine. Footie fans happily adopted these wide-legged pants, but eschewed flares. Flared canvas pants, or 'loons', were associated with hippies – *euch*. As Hunter Davies noted in *The Glory Game* in 1972, 'They don't like being mistaken for hippies, a breed they consider filthy.'

Smooths wore their hair in long, scalloped, shoulder-length phlanges – Rod Stewart meets Mick Ronson – which echoed the long floppy rounded collars of their shirts. As a committed glam-rock devotee, I thoroughly approved of this theatrical development. Though clearly a diluted high-street version of the original Roxy Music/Bowie glam-rock style, smooth seemed like a progressive, positive direction for the hard, hostile, poofter-bashing world of footie. I saw a dim distant light at the end of the tunnel.

The Tartan Army: a smooth apotheosis

Saturday 24 May 1975 is a day that I will never forget, and a day that lots of Scottish footie fans will probably have a hard time remembering. I was working in London as a window dresser at Aquascutum, a Sloaney raincoat shop. (Like Burberry, Aquascutum was one of the many of the posh aristo brands that, as you will see, became associated with the casuals in the following decades. But let's not jump ahead. We are still, chronologically speaking, in the land of the smooths.) I stepped off the bus at Oxford Circus at about 8.30 a.m. Everywhere I looked there were what appeared to be corpses lying in the road. Closer examination revealed them to be Scottish footie fans. Most were comatose, some were making half-hearted efforts to get to their feet. These fans were clearly smooths, but there was a difference. In addition to the wide-legged jeans or pants, Rod Stewart hair and tight 'girlfriend' sweaters, these lads had something very specific going on. Tartan.

The Tartan Army were wrapped, enrobed and adorned with tartan scarves, table runners, knitwear and tablecloths. Here was the kind of flamboyant abandon that is usually reserved for the edgier fashion runways. When, some three years later, Vivienne Westwood and Malcolm McLaren created their tartan-bondage collection – all straps and flying kilts – for their punk store Seditionaries, one could not help but follow a dotted line to the Tartan Army.

Anyone remember The Kilt? This Scottish-themed pub was located on the corner of Brewer Street, directly opposite the side entrance to Aquascutum, or 'Aquascrotum' as it was lovingly redubbed by we employees. Our visual display studio was located directly underneath this tartan-themed watering hole. The stage was set for a deadly encounter. As I rounded the corner into Brewer Street on that fateful May morning, I saw that The Kilt – we are talking the entire pub edifice – was draped with hungover supporters, festooned with mile upon mile of flapping, raging tartan. They looked sensational – terrifying, but also very thirsty.

Stepping over bodies and vomit, I unlocked the door and ran downstairs. Cowering in the staff room I found a colleague named Vanda, who worked on the women's display team. She was hunched over a copy of the *Daily Mail*. According to the paper, the England/ Scotland game – the deciding match of the 1974/75 British Home Championship – would kick off at Wembley at 3 p.m.

Overhead, the fans gradually came to life and began chanting, *'If you hate the f*cking English clap your hands … if you hate the …'*, over and over. Then the stomping started. We smoked fags and made cups of tea and attempted to distract ourselves by organizing the tool closet and the wig cupboard. The chanting and stomping got louder. The ranks of the Tartan Army were swelling. Our teeth began to rattle.

The store manager called at around 11 o'clock. An extra display mannequin was needed in Ladies' Raincoats. We pulled one out of storage, dusted her off and Windexed her hands and face. Vanda

Gary Lineker:

'So Gordon, if you were English, what formation would you play?'

Gordon Strachan:

'If I was English I'd top myself.'

carried the arms and wig and I carried the torso. This was accomplished by grabbing her under the crotch (if you carry a mannequin by the waist the legs fall off). We took a deep breath and opened the studio door.

There is no way to describe the furore that erupted once the (now vast) crowd of Scottish fans clocked our little trio crossing Brewer Street. *Benny Hill* meets *Lord of the Flies*. Most of the comments concerned what the lads would like to do with the bald, defenceless, armless fibreglass female effigy. As soon as the mannequin was dressed and installed, we ran back across the street, this time to shouts of '*jobbie-jabber*' and '*fookin' Sassenach whhoore*' (Vanda hailed from Warsaw).

The following hours remain an anxious blur. I remember that the lads started peeing, in large groups, down our delivery shoot. The initial stream quickly turned into a continuous brook, minus any charming babbling, and began flooding our subterranean lair. We had a choice: get pummelled to death on the street or drown in a Loch Ness of beery urine. Ere long a large lake formed. We called shop security and asked them to come and get us. They gleefully admitted that they were too scared to leave the store.

Our Brewer Street Tartan Army never made it to Wembley. They were either too drunk to find it, or maybe they had eaten their tickets. The game began. Things became marginally quieter. I peeked outside. The Scotsmen were huddled in groups listening to their tinny, tiny trannies.

We ran back downstairs and listened to the game on our radio. Our fate depended on the outcome. Kevin Keegan was the superstar player on the Sassenach team, but the scoring was shared by Gerry Francis (2), David Johnson, Kevin Beattie and Colin Bell. Final score: England 5, Scotland nil. When Aquascutum closed, we fled for our lives towards Regent Street. Nobody chased us. The Tartan Army was too incapacitated by grief and lager to even lob a '*jobbie-jabber*'.

Two years later, back at Wembley, Scotland won the British Home Championship, with Kenny Dalglish and Gordon McQueen scoring the two goals against England's one. The Tartan Army celebrated – The Kilt had wisely changed its name so I am not quite sure of the locus – by invading the pitch and ripping it into chunks with their bare hands so that they could take a piece of the victory field back to Scotland and plonk it in their window boxes and backyards.

The dawn of the casuals

In 1977 hordes of Liverpool supporters – the official Firm name was 'The Urchins' – headed to the continent for the European Cup, subsequently redubbed the UEFA Champions League (remarkably Liverpool won this trophy, and then won it again the following year, and then won it three more times). When those Liverpool Urchins arrived home they were groaning under the weight of looted Euro-swag: Adidas trainers – a Liverpool fave to this day – plus Lacoste and Sergio Tacchini shirts. These undocumented imports had a profound effect on fan style. Casual was born.

The lads now looked spiffy, fresh and, most importantly, unrecognizable to the police. Casual style not only imbued the wearer with a childlike innocence and sweetness – the antithesis of skins and punks – it also provided camouflage. There was something decidedly non-threatening – think Beanie Babies or Teletubbies – about the sight of a group of neatly coiffed casuals, in their V-necks and Golas, on their way to a match.

CASUAL

INFLUENCE AND INSPIRATION

Over the last three-plus decades, casual has been so relentlessly mined, reworked and excavated by the fashion world that it should probably just sit down, enjoy a relaxing cup of tea and a slice of Battenberg cake, and move in. Every designer on Earth has partaken, from biggies like Paul Smith to newbies like Supreme, Christopher Shannon and Gosha Rubchinskiy. In 2015, *ID* magazine began referring to 'the new lad Casual, a style that incorporated skatewear and vintage footie style'. With casual-inspired bands such as The Streets and The Mitchell Brothers, constant references in film and TV – *Green Street, ID, The Firm, The Football Factory* – casual style, in all its nuanced variations, has become something it never intended to be: a gigantic cultural signifier.

Associated magazine editor Allan Kennedy is a former casual and a leading expert on the style. He dissected its various nuances for me as follows:

Argyle: Casuals, mainly working-class boys, plundered the styles of the aristocracy and elites. The casuals adopted the brightly coloured sweaters with argyle patterns that middle-class golfers had worn for years. Posh Scottish knitwear brands like Pringle and Lyle & Scott were mixed with Tacchini tracksuits and Adidas cagoules. They were also influenced by the posh hunting and fishing outfits you'd see on Scottish glens. They even wore Sherlock Holmes deerstalker hats.

Athleisure: Today's trend for athleisure wear is casual's biggest legacy. The casuals were the first to wear a tracksuit in a dressed-up manner. Mixing sportswear garments with denim and knitwear was quite revolutionary at the time.

Layering: Tracksuits were often worn under V-neck sweaters. Also popular: wearing a roll-neck (turtleneck) sweater under a V-neck to create a look that was a play on the old lady 'twinset'.

Hip hop: Casuals made trainers a wardrobe staple. There was a huge similarity between what casuals wore and the emerging Bronx hip hop scene.

Ecstasy: Ecstasy was the ultimate 'love' drug and broke down barriers. For a couple of years we danced with glowsticks and peace reigned, then the more criminal-minded casuals started dealing ecstasy. They were making a lot of money: labels like Stone Island, Timberland, Burberry and Aquascutum started to appear, and a new wave of more hardcore football hooligans emerged.

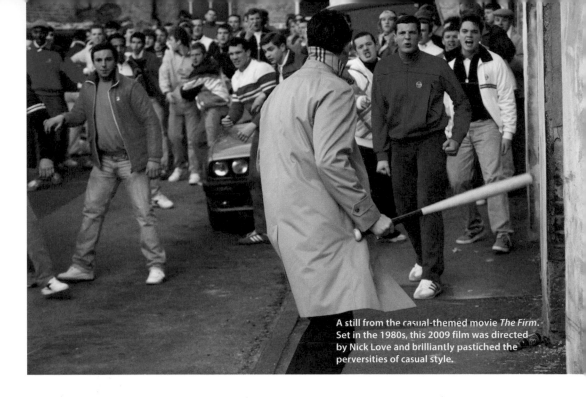

A still from the casual-themed movie *The Firm*. Set in the 1980s, this 2009 film was directed by Nick Love and brilliantly pastiched the perversities of casual style.

The casual look proliferated, adding US and UK brands to the menu, and the police eventually learned that just because someone was wearing Ralph Lauren, Pepe, Benetton, Burberry, Slazenger, Pringle, Stone Island, Fiorucci, Henri Lloyd, Ben Sherman, Fred Perry or Kappa, they should not assume that this particular person was incapable of wielding a baseball bat.

As we have seen, the best footie-fan styles, the most pungent, resonant and redolent, like skin, suede, smooth and casual, are an enduring influence on the men's fashion world. In an era when fashion fetishizes 'street style', why wouldn't designers and stylists harvest inspiration from these spontaneous post-war youth movements? But what about the fans today? What are they actually wearing now?

The golden era of tribal footie-fan fashion has passed. The particular economic and social moments that produced those rage-filled youth cults have passed. However, the styles themselves have *not* passed. Far from it. The fan style worn by the majority of today's fans is a palimpsest of the iconic styles of yore – skin, suede, smooth and casual – dumbed down and diluted with many an anorak. Look closely at the rowdy triangle of travelling fans and you will see faint nods to the fascistic fads of the past: there's always a Fred Perry or two. Adidas and Stone Island are never far off. You might even spot a Baracuta.

THE FUTURE:

Syd Bevers was the most creative and stylish football fan of all time.
Unsurprisingly, he hailed from Blackpool.

Syd Bevers was the founder of the Atomic Boys, an unconventional Blackpool supporters' club which took inspiration from the atomic bomb, as did we all, back in the middle of the last century. His goal was to inject a little *joie de vivre* and Technicolor into post-war footie. At Syd's behest, the Atomic Boys started dressing up: they wore tangerine coats, white trousers and straw hats. Over time these outfits became more ornate and demented. Their accessories included live ducks, dyed orange and smuggled into games with varying degrees of success. If his concealed fowl started quacking at the turnstyles, Syd would start coughing loudly.

Syd's carnivalesque approach to fan style was edged out by malevolent mods and skins. 'It's gone now, mainly because of hooliganism. I wouldn't dare walk about now, in my old outfit, in another town. They'd be after me, wouldn't they?', mused Syd in 1972. Fast forward half a century. The spirit of Syd is *back*.

German fans wear lederhosen and nifty hats. Dutch supporters, typically so reserved and emotionally withholding at Eredivisie games, explode into an orange frenzy of tangerine maquillage and Halloween-esque costumery at international games. Spanish fans favour deconstructed matador outfits, flamenco ruffles and bobble-fringing. An unbridled love of costume can be seen in the stadiums of Europe, America, China, Africa and Latin America.

Nation-inspired fan costumery is creative, fun and kid-friendly. Who wouldn't trade in a horde of menacing Russian Ultras for a group of fun, peace-loving Italians dressed up like pizzas? And if you ever find yourself getting annoyed with some moustachioed bloke in a flamenco frock who insists on thumping his tambourine in your earhole, remember good-hearted, peace-loving Syd, the patron saint of haute couture fan-drag, take a breath and surrender.

PEACE, LOVE ...
AND BOBBLE-FRINGING

Japanese (left) and Italian supporters triumphing over oppressive notions of restraint and 'good taste'.

DR Congo fans doing their best to upstage Ivory Coast rival
supporters at Gabon's Stade Oyem in 2017.

Blackburn fans in 2011, making their feelings about manager Steve Kean known.

'When fans have spent a morning painting slogans on an old picnic blanket, that's when the writing's on the wall. **The tin-tack's just around the corner.**'

Paul Merson

7. Bosses

The Dapper and the Damned

Imagine if every time you show up at work, you are greeted by people waving placards and – yes – jiggling mouldy picnic blankets. Now imagine that the messages on these signs and blankets are all about you, what a useless prat you are and how you should bugger off back where you came from.

To be a football manager is to live with the sword of Damocles hanging above your comb-over. The brutal dynamics of the managerial profession attract strange and extraordinary individuals. These highly idiosyncratic blokes – special ones, gurus, hairdryers, superstitious seers, belligerent nut-jobs, forensic strategists – also have highly idiosyncratic approaches to dressing themselves. In this chapter I will take a sartorial stroll down manager memory lane, and celebrate the styles and quirks of these worshipped and yet much maligned figures.

Plus-fours and spats: the early years

Looking back at the pantheon of football managers from the early days of the game is a bit like staring at a Magritte painting. Who are all these identical, bowler-hatted, black-coated functionaries floating about in the ether? However, upon closer scrutiny, occasional bursts of stylish extroversion can be spotted. Despite the general overarching antipathy of football managers towards fashion, there have always been, even in the olden days, certain individuals whose style was noteworthy and memorable.

With his high Karl Lagerfeld-esque collars, straw boaters and Zapata-on-steroids moustache, Hammers manager Syd King resembled an Edwardian pantomime suitor. He is best remembered for his astounding success managing West Ham, reaching the First Division in the 1926/27 season. According to Tom Fenton in *At Home with the Hammers*, Syd was 'a personality plus man. A man with flare'. Sadly, he took his own life, 'while of unsound mind', by drinking alcohol laced with poison. According to his son, the Hammers' 1932 relegation had triggered a downward spiral. You cannot help wondering if there were picnic blankets involved.

West Ham manager Syd King, c. 1905/6. According to Tom Fenton in *At Home with the Hammers*, Syd was 'a personality plus man. A man with flare'.

Major Frank Buckley, enrobed in tweed and upstaged by matching canine accessories.

Frank Buckley, known as The Major, was a Boer War veteran who went on to manage Blackpool, Wolves and Leeds, all the while wearing his signature plus-fours. A stroppy, charismatic visionary, his innovations were much copied: he started youth programs, his players talked to shrinks to build their confidence, and he made astute buy cheap/sell big transfer decisions. He also increased player flexibility by forcing his lads to participate in dance training, thereby sharpening their competitive edge, not to mention embarrassing the crap out of them. Most important of all, he was the bloke who had the vision to put Blackpool players *in tangerine*.

Above left Exuding portly gravitas, Arsenal's great innovator Herbert Chapman.

Above right Portsmouth manager Jack Tinn, seen here with his valet/spats stylist, in his 'lucky spats'.

Herbert Chapman ruled Arsenal from 1924 to 1935. He introduced the WM formation, he rigged up the first floodlights, he painted footballs white, and he played gramophone records in the dressing room to get players energized (nothing like a scratchy Jessie Matthews 78 to get the juices flowing). Like Major Buckley, Herbert Chapman wore impressive clothes. The old humble, self-effacing manager/secretary was dead and the new, dressed-to-the-nines impresario manager had arrived.

In 1939 Jack Tinn led Portsmouth to FA Cup victory. His team beat Wolves 4:1 at Wembley. Jack Tinn grabbed headlines when he credited the win to his lucky spats.

Jack Cock managed Millwall from 1944 to 1948. 'A sophisticated socialite who dressed in expensive clothes' is

Who said Millwall lack finesse and elegance? Jack Cock, the Lions' sophisticated post-war manager.

how he was described in *The Breedon Book of Football Managers*, while the *Daily Mail* once referred to him as 'tubby manager Jack Cock'. In the twenty-first century, packing on the pounds seems to us like a failing, but back then it augmented Mr Cock's perceived gravitas. Stocky and dapper equalled achievement and success.

With managers like the bespatted Jack Tinn and tweed junkie Frank Buckley we see the advent of something special. By developing a signature flourish these blokes made themselves memorable, and a century later we are still talking about those tweedy plus-fours!

The unswinging Sixties

When the salary cap was lifted in 1961, players suddenly had money to burn on birds, booze and pacey clobber. The Sixties began to unfurl. Did the managers join the fashion Mardi Gras? The notion of Alf Ramsey, Matt Busby or Walter Winterbottom mincing off down the King's Road and plonking down hard-earned cash at Granny Takes a Trip for an embroidered Nehru jacket is delectable,

Matt Busby's dignified style had a tremendous effect on other managers. As Barney Ronay noted in his brilliant book *The Manager: The Absurd Ascent of the Most Important Man in Football*, Busby 'induced a collective doing up of the top button, a sucking in of the gut and a hardening of the ambition'.

1966 World Cup manager Sir Alf Ramsey always dressed impeccably. The dark features that elicited taunts and accusations of gypsy ancestry when he was growing up in Dagenham gave him, once suited and dressed for his managerial responsibilities, the look of an important Hollywood producer like Louis B. Mayer or Samuel Goldwyn. Although Sir Alf's exaggerated sense of propriety sometimes resulted in him adopting a posh accent, he is more often remembered for saying things like 'One of these days I shall lift up a dagger and fuckin' well kill you'.

but sadly the opposite of what was actually going on. The Carnaby carousel began to spin but the managers stayed put. The trendy excesses of the day – not to mention the comportment of the 'fifth Beatle' George Best – only served to convince the managers that this new cult of fashion exhibitionism was threatening, distracting and quite possibly satanic. Managerial responsibilities now included the handling of previously unimagined sums of money. More than ever, the manager's style of dressing needed to telegraph respectability and credibility. Dressing like a flashy strip-club owner or a parvenu turf accountant was simply not going to cut it.

Seventies sartorial bravado, as envisioned by Liverpool legend Bill Shankly.

The Swinging Seventies

In the 1970s, the taboo-busting vibes of the Swinging Sixties filtered down to the general population. Respectable adult males now began to dress with swagger and sass – *If Jimi Hendrix wore a feather boa, then I sure as hell can wear a gaudy kipper tie with a five-inch blade.* Geezer chic was born.

Figures like Bill Shankly, manager of Liverpool from 1959 to 1974, located their inner peacocks and began to fondle them. Suits with six-inch-wide lapels and coloured shirts with cliff-sized collars? Why not? Tie knots as big as your head? Pourquoi pas? La Dolce Vita sunglasses and medallions? Ciao Roma! For these 1970s cult-of-personality managers, dressing like a respectable functionary no longer served any purpose. Instead, dressing like a groovy, swinging, spotlight-seeking international go-getting geezer was where it was at.

Tommy Docherty celebrating the FA Cup victory of his Man Utd side over Liverpool in 1977. His checked suit, cinnamon shirt and spotty tie combo epitomizes the uninhibited theatricality of the '70s manager.

Fedora-wearing Malcolm Allison managed an astounding number of clubs, most notably Manchester City. Mike Summerbee declared him to be 'the best coach this country has ever had'. Big Mal oozed sex appeal. Also of note: he had one lung and once dated Christine Keeler, the centrepiece of the Profumo scandal.

TRACKSUIT TITANS

'**W**hen he reached Stamford Bridge he was ready to be out with his players – one of the breed of tracksuited managers', frothed *The Guardian* of Tommy Docherty in 1967. In the history of manager style, the tracksuit is a chafing, pilling, rash-inducing synthetic constant. Prime ministers come and go, Eurovision winners blossom and fade, but the tracksuit endures. However, over the decades, the symbolism of this brightly coloured, practical garment has changed dramatically.

In the 1950s and 1960s, the wearing of a tracksuit suggested, accurately or not, that the manager in question possessed a degree of dynamism and athleticism. Some managers even kept a tracksuit in their offices, in a drawer, in a plastic bag, just in case a 'see-how-sporty-I-am' photo op materialized. The wearing of a tracksuit, however, is not always intended to suggest athleticism. When Bob Paisley wore his tracksuit, it signified that an intensely analytical approach was in play. Barney Ronay dubs it 'football's equivalent of a lab coat'.

How best might a manager integrate a tracksuit into his sartorial repertoire? Little, if any, thought was given to styling one's tracksuit. The resulting fashion statements were nothing if not memorable. Some managers wore their tracksuits with sheepskin car coats and briefcases. Sunderland's Bob Stokoe teamed his tracksuit – for the FA Cup Final, mark you – with a brown overcoat and a black leather business shoe. This look is so jarringly naff that it almost seems like something Pharrell Williams might sling together in a fit of modish irony.

Today's tracksuit managers – Tony Pulis, Craig Shakespeare, David Wagner et al. – wear their Adidas, Nike and Under Armour with relaxed sporty elan. Accessory crises are, thanks to the explosive proliferation of sneaker styles, a thing of the past. We are in many ways living in the golden age of the tracksuit. Bournemouth's Eddie Howe, for instance, wears his tracksuits with youthful blond aplomb. When appointed in 2009, handsome Eddie became the youngest – and the fittest! – manager in the League. 'I am not a pompous business man', his sporty high-performance garments seem to say.

England Manager Sir Alf Ramsey serving Rat
Pack cool during a training session ahead of the
1970 World Cup tournament in Mexico.

Bob Paisley, taking a no-frills, un-poncy approach.

Brian Clough in 1972, the year that he and legendary sidekick
Peter Taylor led Derby County to their first ever Football
League Championship win. Nothing augurs success quite like
an Umbro-sponsored scrambled-egg yellow tracksuit.

'HE WEARS THE CLUB SHOP, HE WEARS THE CLUB SHOP, TONY PULIS, HE WEARS THE CLUB SHOP.'

Sung by Manchester City fans at Stoke in 2012 – a nod to the fact
that Pulis wore a Stoke tracksuit, trainers and baseball cap.

When bespectacled Jürgen Klopp wears his tracksuit it says, 'I might
wear thick glasses and smoke fags when nobody is looking, but I am
a dynamic motivator and every bit as fit as my lads'.

Bournemouth manager Eddie giving a double teapot.

Ron Atkinson in 1978, during his time at West Bromwich Albion. His *joie de vivre* and love of the finer things in life – he used a sunbed in the office while wearing a thong – earned him the nickname 'Champagne Charlie'. 'The champagne and jewellery image has stuck with me, but it has been perpetuated by people who don't know me. When I was burgled the thieves were gutted not to find my place bulging with gold watches and trinkets', remembers Atkinson, who went on to manage Man Utd to FA Cup wins in 1983 and 1985.

England manager Don Revie with Kevin Keegan (in 22-inch parallels), dodging the paparazzi at Liverpool airport in 1977. When Leeds United mega-manager Revie was annoyed or disappointed with his team, he would enter the changing room, head to the nearest mirror and wordlessly comb (over) his hair.

Tall, regal Hammers legend John Bond (444 appearances)
went on to manage seven clubs including Norwich, Burnley
and Brum. He had two signature flourishes: his spotless belted
raincoats and that impressive bouffant hairdo.

Dignified and double-breasted, George
Graham pays his respects to his legendary
Gunners predecessor.

The Savile Row gang: a return to tradition

The 1980s saw a dramatic end to geezer chic. Charged with ever larger responsibilities, the manager scrambled to put the free-wheeling flamboyance of the 1970s behind him. He began to dress with gravitas and sartorial restraint … or like a bank manager. The flamboyant fedoras and jangling man-jewellery of the 1970s quickly became a huge source of mockery and cringing fashion regret. Cries of 'What the hell were we thinking?' filled the air.

The Eighties saw the rise of Ralph Lauren and the fetishization of patrician style and poshness. Dignity and elegance abounded. As an example, look no further than Arsenal managing legend George Graham. Paul Merson remembers him swanning about, 'jumper draped over his shoulders like Prince Charles on a summer stroll'. In *Fever Pitch*, Nick Hornby describes Graham as 'an upright, immaculately groomed, handsome man, with an obvious taste for expensive well-cut formal clothes'.

Looking dignified comes at a cost, but managers were making plenty of coin. Time to ditch Marks & Spencer and head straight to Savile Row. The managers of the Eighties and Nineties began to build wardrobes of classic custom-made, bespoke, hand-stitched elegance. This was the era of *Wall Street*'s Gordon Gecko, and footie was becoming big business. As the sums of money involved soared through the roof, so did the need to look like you could handle it.

Not only were the managers dealing with increased business pressures, they were also dealing with players whose wheels were well and truly coming off. Lads like Paul Merson, Tony Adams and Paul Gascoigne were finding new and ever more creative ways to break taboos, while emptying their bank accounts. All the more reason for the managers of the day – Robson, Wenger, Taylor, Hoddle – to dress with unimpeachable rectitude. Unimpeachable rectitude sounds like something that might happen after you sat too long on a cold stadium seat, but it is the phrase that best describes the doggedly dignified style which emerged

Dapper Fergie and gaga Gazza.

In the coming decades the vast majority of UK managers signed on to the Savile Row look: Mark Hughes, Roy Keane, Alan Pardew (above left), Phil Brown, Sam Allardyce, Sean Dyche, Brendan Rodgers (above right) … the list goes on.

as the twentieth century screeched to a close, and football managers started dressing like George W. Bush.

What are the key components of this enduring and classic style? First and foremost we have the bone-crushingly expensive bespoke suit, in dark grey or navy. Not too fitted. Centre vent. Two button. Low armhole. Flat-front cuffless pant. Trouser width neither too narrow nor not wide. The perfect shirt: no trippy '70s colour combos. Subtly striped, but most often white. Pristine. Starched. Not button-down. Slightly spread collar, but nothing crazy. Remarkably unremarkable. The presidential tie, blue or red, occasionally striped. Never snazzy. No big knots. No small knots. No tiepins. No giant watches. No douchey cufflinks, bracelets or Liberace pinky rings. No dramatic chapeaux. And never *ever* an umbrella.

When, in 2007, Steve McClaren carried a large red and navy golfing umbrella onto the Wembley pitch, he instantly became 'the Wally with the Brolly', an early social media punching bag. When Steve's lads lost to Croatia, thereby failing to qualify for Euro 2008, Steve lost his job. His hokey brolly became a horrible symbol of failure. It was the opposite of Mary Poppins.

Learning to tone it down

In his autobiography Sir Alex Ferguson talks, revealingly, about his publicity learning curve. When first dealing with the press back in the early days he felt a natural obligation to feed the media a sassy or memorable headline. Once the social media revolution rolled into town, he quickly learned that the obligation to give a pungent quote was no longer serving the interests of the club. Deliver a cheeky bon mot and it will be seized upon, taken out of context and used to mock all concerned.

The same learning arc can be applied to manager clothing. The 1970s was a time to show off and make an impression with bold colours and wide lapels. This is no longer a valid approach for managers. Wear something noteworthy, and the press will 'wally your brolly' till it hurts. By dressing with unimpeachable rectitude – nothing quirky or noteworthy *ever*! – Fergie and the British managers who continue the Savile Row tradition successfully deprive the media of the opportunity to hate upon their attire and, more importantly, on them.

Sven-Göran Eriksson: the Swede with the look of a bespoke British bank manager.

Arsène Wenger OBE has been managing Arsenal since 1996. He may have brought continental ideas about training and nutrition, but his personal style is now doggedly Anglophilic. No berets and matelot tops for him.

The Eurofabulous style icons

Classic Savile Row Brits and Eurofabulous managers like Antonio Conte and Pep Guardiola hail from two totally different tribes. While the Brit manager strives for classic conservatism, the more fashionable Euro-manager prefers Italian designer clothing that is graphic, edgy and monochromatic.

Eight out of 20 current Premier League managers are British. The rest are mostly Eurofabulous. The difference between the UK classicists and the Eurofabulous designer-clad managers is Mayfair versus Milan. It's formal versus designer-casual. Eurofabulous managers buy their cashmere V-necks and cardies and their

Pep Guardiola of Manchester City (right) and Chelsea's Antonio Conte definitely dress like managers ... managers of a trendy boutique hotel, or maybe the Prada store in Milan.

Clockwise from top left Hervé Renard;
Quique Sánchez Flores;
Zinedine Zidane; Joachim Löw

unlined navy sports jackets at Armani, Cucinelli, Hermès, Loro Piana, Prada and Zegna. Their suits, if they wear them at all, are tighter and spiffier. Ties are narrower. The only flamboyance is the occasional addition of a szhooshy scarf – cashmere in winter, silk and linen in summer.

There are a couple of interesting exceptions. Argentinian Mauricio Pellegrino (Southampton) and Portuguese Marco Silva (Watford) reject Eurofabulosity, dressing instead with the studied indifference of a Brummy geography teacher circa 1980. At the other end of the style spectrum we have Swansea City's Paul Clement, one of the spiffiest managers in the 2017/18 season, and a bloke who has spent much of his career in Europe. As a result he eschews that British classicism, choosing instead the Eurofabulous designer style of Pep, Conte and Zidane, thereby resembling a very stylish undertaker. (Pep postscript: just before this book went to print, Pep Guardiola suddenly and shockingly traded in his formal spiffy attire for skinny jeans, sportif tops and casual blouson jackets. This sartorial complacency is, in my opinion, a direct function of how well his team is doing in the current 2017/18 season, i.e. very well. My prediction: if the Man City lads start to falter, he will be back in those undertaker suits quicker than you can say Abu Dhabi.)

Cremation or burial, madam? Paul Clement serving European funeral parlour chic, at Swansea City.

Managers are mysterious blokes. But José Mourinho – or Maureen, as I like to call him – might just be the most enigmatic specimen of all time. On 27 April 2015, days before Chelsea became Premier League champions, and about six months before Maureen led her lads off a cliff, he gave an interview to style website Mr Porter. Nestling among some moody snapshots of our Maur – enrobed in an array of outrageously expensive Eurofabulous knitwear – I unearthed the following nugget: 'I would never wear a red shirt or a red blazer. Or a yellow tie. No, I just like to wear grey, blue, light blue, dark blue, white … you open my wardrobe, and you see white, grey, blue, light blue, dark blue.' The enigmas and mysteries of the Maureen legend are hauntingly illustrated in this melancholic haiku. Dark blue and light blue, yes, of course. But red? No, never (the

SIR PAUL SMITH
reflects on Mourinho, Hoddle and Armani:

I am currently working with José Mourinho on suits for Manchester United. I have dressed lots of teams over the years. It's always a challenge, but fun. It gets a bit tricky when managers get too involved and start having opinions, especially about colour. I always want to put the players in navy or grey. The reason is simple. There's a big range of people who have to be fitted: masseurs, doctors, physios, all shapes and sizes, not just footballers, who are so easy to dress. One time Glenn Hoddle wanted pale beige. Imagine all those different bodies, in *beige*! I compromised. We ended up with taupe.

Years ago Armani designed suits for Liverpool. He wanted to make a big statement so he did white. Everyone made fun of the players and the staff: *'Ere! Can I buy an ice cream?*

José Mourinho, currently at Manchester United, is the king of Eurofabulosity.

Red Devils? Never?). And, no, not yellow … Subtext: I will never be the manager of Norwich or Watford.

Full disclosure: Mourinho is not the only top-flight manager for whom I have concocted a female nickname. Other examples include Polly Pardew, Samantha Allardyce, Granny Pellegrini, Jolene Klopp, etc., etc. Funnily enough, I have never felt the impulse to dub the players, or the refs, or the owners, with women's names. But the managers … why *wouldn't* you replace Louis van Gaal with 'Dutch Dora'? The manager role is nothing if not womanly, and maternal. Even though managers like to think of themselves as Big Daddy, we all know that they are really Big Mummy. I have tremendous respect for the mummies of the world. It's a thankless, difficult job. Look at them go, cheering on the sidelines like pageant moms, doling out discipline and guidance, alternating between smacks and kisses, reinforcing good behaviour and generally trying to keep the whole brood on the straight and narrow. Go Maureen!

The WAG-ristocracy: a competent, calm and collected Coleen Rooney, emerging from Claridges.

> 'I predict that ninety-nine percent of WAGs meet their footballers out on the piss. The remaining one percent met their footballers at school, were childhood sweethearts who grew up together – **if it can be said that footballers do grow up.'**
>
> *I Am The Secret Wag*

8. WAGs

The Worthy and the Wag-tastic

What kind of women do footballers prefer? A more apropos question might be 'what kind of women prefer footballers?' With a cursory look at the football landscape, the truth is quickly revealed: footballers are the hunted, rather than the hunter.

As Peter Crouch quipped in 2007, back when he was playing for Liverpool, 'What would I have been if I hadn't become a footballer? A virgin.' Among today's diverse tribes of modern women, there remains a certain type of lass who is disinclined towards sensitive, vegan, poetic types. These chicks view footballers as hyper-masculine, exciting, reckless, and therefore desirable. When *EastEnders* actress Danniella Westbrook announced, 'I like a bit of rough – footballers, roofers, blokes who get banged up', she showed us that Chippendales porn fantasies are alive and well in the contemporary female imagination. And then there's the dosh. Abbey Clancy, Mrs Peter Crouch, once declared that her ambition was to 'marry a footballer, get pregnant, and then shop and have fun'. She is not unusual. Materialism and hedonism are the cornerstones of WAG-dom.

Above Headed up the shops, the England WAGs of the 2006 World Cup form a phalanx on the streets of Baden Baden. 'Reservoir Wags' screeched one unforgettable headline.

Left Crouch and Clancy. Finding a rich husband is a time-honoured tactic for women in search of a pampered life. Abbey Clancy and the girls have breathed new life into this age-old strategy.

Looking at it from the WAG's point of view, it all makes perfect sense. More than ever, women are bombarded with images of glamour, porn, celebrity and wealth. How might a regular girl from a small town attempt to sync up her life with the swanky cavalcade of pampering, sexting and luxury that unfurls daily on her social media feeds? Marry a footballer.

The WAG phenomenon first reared its extension-encrusted head at the 2006 World Cup in Germany. The media had a field day covering the English wives and girlfriends, including – but not limited to – Victoria Beckham, Cheryl Tweedy, Coleen McLoughlin, Abbey Clancy, Alex Curran, Elen Rivas, and honorary WAG Nancy Dell'Olio, who was in a highly publicized relationship with manager Sven-Göran Eriksson at the time. While the players trained, the WAGs quaffed poolside cocktails and conspired with the press. The hotel management erected a screen so the WAGs could sunbathe without being papped, but the WAGs insisted on its removal.

Overnight, WAGs became objects of fascination, envy and ridicule. Call it a WAG-lash. Everyone had a go at the WAGs, even the WAGs themselves: 'These women don't cook for their husbands, they don't clean, they have all the handbags they want,' kvetched pop singer Cheryl Tweedy (Cole), adding, 'but they never do a day's work. What kind of aspiration is that?' The lightning-rod WAGs checked all the boxes of the emerging reality-show culture:

celebrity, wealth, sex and, most important of all, the Kardashian box. They embodied the fantasy *du jour*: doing bugger all but still living the life of Riley.

In the intervening years the world of WAGs has grown and diversified. Some of today's WAGs are mega-WAGs, and some are earnest to the point of barely being WAG-y at all. Melanie Slade-Walcott is a good example of the latter. Theo Walcott's missus and childhood sweetheart is a wholesome girl who does not court the spotlight. Stine Gyldenbrand is married to Leicester City goalie Kasper Schmeichel, with whom she has two children. No lingerie model she. Being a hard-working professional midwife makes her significantly less WAG-y than fellow Foxes glamour-WAGs Rebekah Vardy, Rita Mahrez and Leah Richards, fiancée to Matty James.

At the other end of the WAG spectrum, we have the *grandes horizontales*, the WAGs who are so WAG-alicious that they *only* date footie players. Lingerie model Vanessa Perroncel, for example, is what you might call a real WAG's WAG. Among her many conquests she is alleged to have dallied with five Chelsea players (separately), including John Terry and Adrian Mutu. Gorgeous

Nuremberg rally, starring Cheryl Tweedy and Victoria Beckham.

Djibril Cissé's 2005 fairytale wedding – he married a hairdressing consultant from Anglesey named Jude – saw him totally upstage his WAG by donning an Edwardian blood red frock-coated tuxedo. His wife subsequently got her revenge, post-divorce, by appearing with the kids on an episode of *Britain's Flashiest Families*.

Raffaella Fico is the daughter of Italian fruit and veg sellers. Cristiano Ronaldo and Mario Balotelli have both scrawled their names on her dance card. Mariana Paesani, another 'lingerie model', dated Carlos Tevez, among others. Which others? I'll let La Paesani answer that question: 'I die for footballers. When I want a player I simply become a goddess. I cover myself with vanilla and chocolate essence so they want to eat me whole.'

And then there are the ladies who are post-WAG. Victoria Beckham no longer qualifies as a WAG, since her husband is now retired. But even when David was playing she was, paradoxically, never a very WAG-y WAG. Ironic, really, to think that the girl who inspired a generation of WAG-olytes turns out to have drifted from the pack. Victoria is too entrepreneurial, hard-working, creative and accomplished to be a lifelong WAG. Being a member of the biggest-selling girl group of all time, and then going on to found an eponymous global fashion brand? And receiving an OBE? Disqualified!

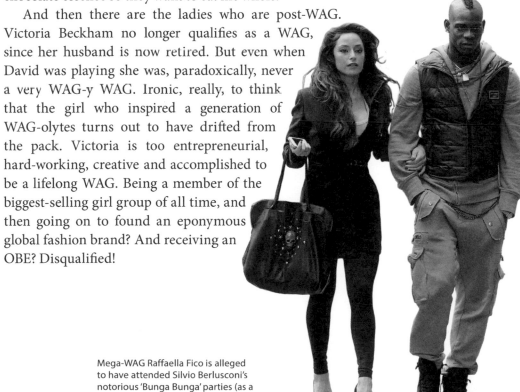

Mega-WAG Raffaella Fico is alleged to have attended Silvio Berlusconi's notorious 'Bunga Bunga' parties (as a casual observer, of course).

Worthy WAGs of yore

Footballers have always had wives and girlfriends, but over the last couple of decades the explosion in salaries, rampant materialism, the new obsession with designer fashion and accessories, and the uncontained, raving, spewing madness of internet-fuelled celebrity culture have transformed the nature of WAG-dom beyond all recognition. It is important to hit the mute button every once in a while, to remember that it was not always thus, and to pay homage to the worthy, humble WAGs of yesteryear.

Ever heard of Viv Neate? In WAG history, this footie folk-heroine deserves a mention and possibly a statue outside my home-town stadium. Mrs Neate, a salt-of-the-earth early WAG, was married to Gordon Neate, a 1960s Reading player turned head groundsman. Viv washed the Reading kit, including undies, every week for 20 years and dried it in her backyard. She persuaded her neighbour to take out a section of fence so that she could extend her washing line. Viv would incentivize the players by threatening to withhold the conditioner: 'Play well and you'll get Comfort in your socks!'

Though most twentieth-century WAGs were not scrubbing kit, they were far from pampered. WAGs like Judith Hurst, wife

Looking at the World Cup WAGs of 1966 in their nylons and respectable fashions, it's hard to believe that these demure girls were the antecedents for today's vajazzlers.

Something about the Hurst kiddies' fashions screams 'home dressmaking'. Hard to imagine today's WAGs grabbing the pinking shears and pedalling the Singer.

of World Cup hat-tricker Geoff Hurst, led lives of service, sequestered at home, minding the sprogs. They were allowed out to watch the games, where their primary role was to demonstrate ferocious WAG loyalty. Judith recalled how she used to 'stand up and glare around when fans were giving Geoff stick'.

Tina Moore, the first media-friendly footballer's wife, was a magical mix of Sixties dolly bird and loving spouse. Eighteen months before the miraculous England World Cup win of 1966, she nursed captain Bobby through cancer, chemo and testicle removal. Bobby and Tina, relatable and yet slightly out of reach, were like a beautiful idealized version of a young English working-class married couple. As a result, people wanted to *be* them. They were the canary in the coalmine for Posh and Becks.

Meanwhile, across the channel, Johan Cruyff was penniless when Diana Margaretha 'Danny' Coster agreed to marry him, so he borrowed the dough to pay for their wedding. Pictures of the occasion suggest that it was by no means a budget affair. It is hard to imagine today's WAGs marrying a bloke who had to plunge into debt in order to fund the occasion, but the proof was in the *appeltaart*. The Cruyffs endured for almost half a century, with Danny at Johan's bedside when he died of lung cancer in 2016, aged 68.

Bound for the 1970 Mexico World Cup: Mrs Bobby Moore, Mrs Geoffrey Hurst, Mrs Martin Peters and Mrs Peter Bonetti. The pleasing diversity of styles – pantsuits to party dresses – suggests that the ladies conferred about their outfits ahead of time.

Today's moneyed footballers spoil their WAGs with Hermès Birkin bags and vats of perfume. For the Tinas of the last century, luxuries were few and far between. In 1972 Spurs' Mike England returned from Romania bearing gifts: a couple of watercolours in gilt frames (it's the thought that counts). According to Spurs chronicler Hunter Davies, 'The rest of the players brought back fluffy dolls'. Every expense was spared.

By the 1970s the media spotlight was increasingly focused on the nation's top footballers and their loved ones. The uninvited attention did not always sit well with yesterday's wives and girl-friends. Ann Bowles was married to QPR badboy legend Stan Bowles during his '70s heyday. The burgeoning sizzle and atten-tion – so intoxicating to many of today's WAGs – irritated the crap out of honest Ann: 'I don't think people realize what it's like being a footballer's wife', she told the press at the time, adding, 'It's get-ting on my nerves. He gets all these invites, and the phone keeps ringing all the time.' The invites were arriving and the times were a-changing. Something was blowing in the wind, and it smelled a lot like Chanel No. 5. Goodbye Viv. Hello Chardonnay.

'In our day the players didn't earn big money and women weren't attracted to them because they had huge amounts of money, but that seems to be what girls aspire to these days.'

Tina Moore to *The Sun*, 2016

The wedding of Johan Cruyff and Danny Coster: Johan is in a tailcoat looking like an Eton prefect, while Danny, regal and very 1967, sports a massive hairdo of cartoonish tunnel-curls, à la Sharon Tate when she married Roman Polanski.

WAG style

Today's WAGs and their style are a clear manifestation of foot-ballers' desires and tastes. The majority of WAGs, just like their husbands and boyfriends, are fundamentally conventional. WAGs are not fashion rule-breakers. Most WAGs don't do freaky. In all my wanderings I only found one WAG who favours eccentric styles: Ivone Viana, wife of Portuguese midfielder and Psychedelic Ninja Raul Meireles, who shares her husband's passionate commitment to edgy clothing, rampant ink and road-warrior coiffures.

The average WAG has an uncomplicated, predictable relation-ship with fashion. With her heels, hyper-femininity, La Dolce Vita lifestyle and luscious figure, the wiggling WAG is reminiscent of vintage movie stars like Gina Lollobrigida and Liz Taylor. The goal of the WAG is twofold: to look expensive and, most importantly, to look HOT.

When Victoria Beckham made her move on the fashion world, she toned down the hotness and expensive designer flash, and amped up a more nuanced, high-fashion, sophisticated, *Vogue*-appropriate

From pop star to fashion star: Victoria Beckham offers a definitive demonstration of the transformative power of style.

look. Stylistically she went from a 'what-men-want' look to more of a 'what-Anna-Wintour-wants' look. The goal? To establish herself as a credible fashion authority with an idiosyncratic POV. Credit where credit is due, she has achieved her goal. Full disclosure: I work for a company that enthusiastically purveys the Victoria Beckham collection and have attended many VB shows and hung out with her on several occasions. She is funny, unpretentious and irreverent, and deserves every stitch of her success.

Back to WAG style: how to look expensive? In WAG-world this is achieved through the acquisition of Chanel/Hermès/Gucci handbags, designer schmattas and 24-carat canary yellow diamonds. It is also achieved through meticulous coiffing, laser teeth-whitening, Botox, Saint Tropez spray tans and dramatic maquillage, which includes thick foundation, thicker eyebrows, eyelash extensions and, for special occasions, individually applied fake lashes. Et voilà! The expensive *poule de luxe*!

Looking hot is a more complicated undertaking than looking expensive. WAGs must always combine sexiness with restraint. They must avoid anything that might be construed as cheap, desperate or obvious. Super-slutty outfits are associated with WAG-wannabes, the girls who are trying to steal their husbands and boyfriends and who stagger around Albert Square ranting and raving after a night on the lash. WAGs achieve hotness by working out on a daily basis and then showcasing the results in expensive frocks by designers like Azzedine Alaïa, Hervé Leger and Dolce & Gabbana. If their figures are not sufficiently curvaceous, they will achieve hotness through surgical intervention.

> 'It's incredible that she has left me. Only recently I paid £7,000 to make her breasts bigger – and now this.'
>
> Hanover striker Mo Idrissou speaking about his ex-girlfriend in 2004

I Am The Secret WAG, the rejoinder to the *I Am The Secret Footballer* book series and *Guardian* column, provides endless insights regarding the lengths that WAGs will go to in order to achieve hotness. The Secret WAG is candid about her own shortcomings, especially the fact that she is lacking in the boob department. The WAGs in her orbit out-knocker her at every turn. At first she tries stuffing her bra with gel pads. This ends in catastrophe when one of the pads falls out of her dress and lands on the dancefloor. An adjacent reveller skids on it and nearly breaks his neck. An onlooker picks it up and asks her, 'Is this your chicken fillet?'

Ivone Viana and Raul
Meireles, God bless 'em,
are lost in a fabulous
fashion *folie-a-deux*.

When childbirth turns her small breasts into 'skanky old tea-bags', the Secret Wag decides to take action. Breast implants take her from a 32A to a happy, buoyant 32C (it's hard to believe that she did not go larger, but since she is the Secret Wag, there is no way to determine whether she's fibbing).

And now for the non-surgical *pièce de résistance*, the signature WAG flourish, the icing on the WAG. I refer to the fashion accessory that combines both hotness and expensiveness: *heels*. WAGs always seal the deal with sky-high stilettos, from Louboutin and Blahnik to Jimmy Choo. Designer shoes are the lynchpin of the WAG look, communicating, as they do, both richesse and porno-hotness.

MADONNA

AND CHILD

When a footballer and his WAG appear in public – it could be a trip to Selfridges or maybe one of those smart/casual team dinners – something strange happens which needs to be underscored. These glamorous couples are, in many ways, a study in contrasts. The busty WAGs, with their heavy, aggressive make-up, blown-out hair and designer bags, tend to look older than their years. There is something Real Housewife-ish and grown-up about the polished predatory glamour of all that expensive hotness. Their footballers, on the other hand, are trending in the opposite direction. They adopt a youthful, playful sporty style. Yes, there are a few Good Taste Ambassadors, but most players opt for a more juvenile POV: we're talking graphic T-shirts, blouson jackets, squeaky-clean trainers, backpacks and ripped punk-inspired jeans. As a result, if you saw a footballer couple in the distance and your eyesight was a bit iffy, you might well mistake them for a milf-and-son combo.

What does this signify? There is no question in my mind that footballers, with their tendency towards arrested development – no offence! – are in dire need of a mother figure. Once a WAG goes from girlfriend to wife, she must take on a more complex adult maternal role. Dressing like a hipster waif or an ingénue would not serve her interests. Her husband can get away with appearing like a skateboarding teen, but the WAG needs to adopt a more take-charge womanly appearance if she is going to keep her footballer in line.

Mother and son? Not so fast: gorgeous singing WAG Lorelei Taron is two years younger than her 31-year-old boy-toy/husband Radamel Falcao. The AS Monaco striker's choice of Little Lord Fauntleroy evening slippers only adds fuel to the May/December fire. Conclusion: players dress with youthful bad-boy swagger, while WAGs opt for the gravitas and glamour which befit their supervisory maternal role.

I shop therefore I WAG

WAGs, in all their expensive and hot finery, are manifestations of footballer taste. But there is reciprocity. WAGs also help to shape the tastes of their men. How? Shopping.

The word 'shopping' appears on the pages of *I Am The Secret WAG* a staggering 26 times. Just to give a little perspective, the word 'vagina' appears only five times, 'Ferrari' appears three times and 'penis' appears once. WAGs have established shopping as a legit, relationship-nourishing couples' activity. Requiring both commitment and enthusiasm, shopping is up there with shagging and vacationing. It is during these endless WAG-propelled retail forays that the footie players are exposed to new fashion trends, developing their sense of style in the process.

'It was Milan and Prada, or Sunderland and Primark.'

Sunderland manager, Steve Bruce, in 2010 after reports that he was hoping to sign Beckham (Mr and Mrs Beckham opted for the better shopping of Milan)

The major cities of Europe are strewn with high-priced shops that cater to the needs and increasingly fashiony tastes of the footballers and WAGs. During these ritualized excursions, under the watchful eye of the WAG, the lad figures out which tribe – Good Taste Ambassador, Label King, Psychedelic Ninja, Hired Assassin, Bohemian or Fauxhemian – is right for him, and then, with repeated outings, he hones his style, usually at great expense.

Private dressing rooms are the norm. These szhooshy suites are equipped with fully stocked bars and various distracting toys. For the kids? Apparently not. A fashion insider who had visited Harvey Nichols in Brum, and who spoke to me on the condition of absolute anonymity, assured me that these toys were in the celeb dressing room 'because of the players' short attention spans'.

Player turned manager Andriy Voronin and his WAG doing some damage during his time at Liverpool.

The good, the bad and the WAG-ly

WAGs are, in many ways, a microcosm of contemporary mores. The obsession with celebrity, money, social media and flawless physicality all reach a screeching crescendo in the WAG. The self-critical impulses that now dog regular chicks are far greater for the always-being-scrutinized competitive WAG. Not only does she compare herself to other WAGs, she also compares herself to her man. A shared anxiety about physical beauty ping pongs back and forth between the godlike footie player and his WAG: 'The knock-on effect of having someone like him around me for years is that I too have exhaustingly high-maintenance health, fitness, grooming and dieting habits', observes the Secret Wag.

Being a top-shelf WAG is not an easy life. Between raising kids, looking gorgeous, dealing with immature over-sexed partners who retire at 35, and those hordes of envious online trolls, WAG lives are about as tranquil as a North London derby. Respect is thin on the ground. The fashion world, in particular, is not nearly as appreciative of the WAGs as it should be. They are seen as déclassé. No designer is clamouring to throw free frocks at a WAG. But WAGs take the high road. When others go low, they go high. Their response is very commendable: *they open their handbags and they pay full retail.* WAGs and footie players, therefore, will always be the most genuine of fashion patrons and should be treated with the utmost respect. *More toys in dressing room #3!* By spending freely, the lads and their WAGs feed the economy. Much of that absurd dough that pours into the players' pockets – in ever increasing amounts – goes back into circulation, thereby supporting fashion businesses (not to mention William Hill) and creating jobs.

There is an erroneous impression that WAG-world is waning. It is true that the media coverage of WAGs is not quite as frenzied as it was in the Noughties. Brand managers and PR gurus now actively dissuade couples from inflaming social media with the kind of mental displays of conspicuous consumption that we saw in Baden Baden. But WAG will out. Unless managers start castrating their players, there will always be wives and girlfriends, and they will always get their WAG on. For every new Marcus Rashford or Harry Winks there is a newly minted WAG waiting in the wings.

Postscript: WAG-watchers went into a frenzy when, in late September 2017, England national team manager Gareth Southgate announced that WAGs would, for the first time since the distracting-but-magical WAG-fest of 2006, be welcome to attend the 2018 FIFA World Cup in Russia. It's a win win. The Moscow fashion retailers will get a much-needed bump and, if England tank, Southgate will have the perfect scapegoat.

Historically, both clubs and players were reticent to cash in on the financial potential of football. And then everyone – not just Gary Lineker and his crisps – figured it out, big time.

'When the business is more important than the football, I don't care. I just gave up. I don't want to be treated like a pair of socks, a shirt, like shit. **I'm not shit.**'

Eric Cantona in 2002, offering insights into the reasons for his sudden 1997 retirement

9. The Big Shill

How Football Learned to Cha-ching

Today's football world is rancid with gruesome stories of bungs, leveraged buy-outs, asset-stripping and off-shore tax fiddles. But when the stench of financial opportunism gets too much, it's good to remind yourself that football, for its first 100 years, did a spectacular job of keeping capitalist assaults at bay.

Corporate logos, for example, did not appear on club shirts until Liverpool hooked up with Hitachi in 1979. A genteel, anti-prof-iteering philosophy was enshrined in the very constitution of football at the dawn of the twentieth century: rule 34 in the Football Association handbook specifically states that football clubs exist to foster the sport, not to make money for any so-called 'owners'. Fiercely protective of the working-class, humble roots of their beautiful game, the club secretaries, managers and directors of the past worked hard to make sure their clubs remained untainted by the painful sight of brimming coffers, or any coffers at all.

And what of the players? What about their coffers? Were they reticent to cash in on their individual charisma and fabulosity? Yes … and then, ever so much, no.

From budgies to boutiques

Vintage football annuals from the 1960s and '70s show players engaged in a variety of non-lucrative pastimes, many of which are so heartbreakingly earnest they seem more like occupational therapy than anything that might constitute fun for a young lad at the height of his throbbing manhood. Everton's Eddie Wainwright reduced post-game stress by growing chrysanthemums, while Man City's Roy Little surrendered to the joys of marquetry. Animals often figured in players' extramural activity choices. Bristol City's Ray Savino was a self-described 'rabbit fancier' and Southampton's Terry Paine was a 'poodle enthusiast', both of which sound like euphemisms for some kind of terrifying perversion. Unfortunately this was not the case.

Budgerigars were the most popular hobby-critter. Not very high maintenance or time-consuming, unless you decide, as many footie players did, that these colourful birds needed to be taught how to chirp out their own names. Contemporary players, with their million-dollar licensing deals, would be aghast at the dorkiness, the wasted time, and the fact that these players were, in some cases, actually *spending* money on their non-money-making hobbies. That birdseed and cuttlefish was not going to purchase itself! Soon the penny would drop … literally.

Still flogging those suede trenches, in 1969 Bobby Moore took his teammates and the press on a factory tour.

In 1972 Spurs defender Maurice Norman did something it is safe to say that Carlos Tevez or Mario Balotelli will never do: he opened a wool shop in Frinton. One can only imagine the frenzy on pension day, with hordes of oldsters clamouring to buy a few skeins of tangerine angora from the local celebrity footballer.

'I'm a numismatist', declares Chelsea's Ian Hutchinson in a 1970 annual. In the interview Ian talks about the value of his rare coin collection and the money that can be made from re-selling coins. Sheesh! Finally! A glimmer of entrepreneurial zeal. A little recognition that careers are short and that making dough while the sun shines might not be such a bad idea after all.

In the 1970s more and more footie players began ditching their twee hobbies in order to 'start a business'. Liverpool's Peter Thompson cut the ribbon on a garage, brimming with Ford Cortinas. Chelsea's Barry Bridges opened a (slightly sordid-looking) hotel with his father-in-law. These optimistic young lads flung themselves into these money-burning ventures with a commendable mixture of optimism, naivety and grandiosity. Unsurprisingly, success was spotty.

For footballers in the second half of the last century, the word 'boutique' vibrated with possibilities. As we have seen, George Best and Mike Summerbee were the first to open and close high-profile fashion boutiques. Their lack of success did nothing to dim the retailing enthusiasms of other players.

Undeterred by the obvious challenges of retail, Kenny Dalglish opened and closed a boutique named 'Dalglish' and Malcolm Macdonald graced Newcastle, albeit briefly, with an eponymous emporium of elegance. 'It was imaginatively named Malcolm Macdonald', recalled Harry Pearson in *The Guardian* in 2003, 'and sold jackets with lapels the size of the Titanic. Unfortunately it sank almost as fast.' The boutique madness continued into the

Nineties. Middlesbrough midfielder Jamie Pollock at least had the decency not to name his boutique 'Jamie Pollock', opting instead for the more enigmatically chic name 'Classified'.

The whole notion of footie players opening fashion boutiques loomed so large on the cultural landscape that it once became fodder for a Monty Python sketch featuring Eric Idle as an extremely nelly interviewer and John Cleese as a braindead footballer named Buzzard:

> *Interviewer*: 'Were you not surprised at the way the Italian ceded midfield dominance so early on in the game?'
>
> *Buzzard (after an excruciating pause)*: 'Well Brian …
> I'm opening a boutique.'

David Beckham spokesmodelling for Adidas in 1997.
By 2003 the footie star's total annual income was
£10 million. £3 million came from licensing deals
with Adidas, Brylcreem and Marks & Spencer.

A licence to shill

Footballers eventually realized that launching a business or opening a boutique was not quite the lottery win they had imagined, but that real money could be made simply by licensing the use of one's name. Flogging their image involved no investment. All you had to do was to try not to lose any front teeth in bar fights and to show up and pose for a few daft pictures. The range of products that footie players now began to promote is staggering. 'I even did an ad for Playtex bras, but not modelling one I hasten to add', recalled George Best in his memoir.

Franz Beckenbauer in 1976, flogging a device named the 'Hairmatic' clipper. Designed to both style and trim, the Hairmatic was conceived by Der Kaiser himself, in an attempt, one assumes, to gain the upper hand with those Brillo-pad locks. Autographed and boxed, vintage Hairmatics can be purchased on eBay for as little as €75.

During his career Kevin Keegan flogged everything from Lyons Maid ice lollies to a 'tension-releasing' fragrance called *Je L'aimerai*. His branding journey reached its apex when, in 1972, he lensed a steamy, bro-tastic Brut 33 deodorant ad with boxing superstar Henry Cooper. Journalist Harry Pearson calls it 'the most notoriously disturbing shower scene since *Psycho*'.

Footballers quickly discovered that the world of licensing and spokesmodelling, though ridiculously lucrative, is not all chuckles and moonbeams. When '70s star Stan Bowles signed two mega boot deals, the QPR maverick felt like he had won the pools. When his English international teammates asked him how he intended to fulfil his dual branding obligations, funster Bowles replied 'For £450 I'll wear one boot on each foot'. And this is exactly what he did, severely aggravating both Gola and Adidas in the process.

After becoming a lachrymose folk hero at the 1990 World Cup semi-final against West Germany, Paul Gascoigne was deluged with offers to promote various products. When he scores a million-dollar Brut aftershave deal, he cannot believe his good fortune. All he has to do is shoot a few ads, and then show up at the press conference. Simple enough, right?

> 'How long have you been using Brut?'
> 'I don't.'
> 'What aftershave do you use then, Paul?'
> 'None. They bring me out in a rash.'

Contract cancelled.

After appearing in an ad for a big mobile phone company, Franz Beckenbauer specifically requested the number 0176 666666 for his new mobile phone. His instrument was soon blowing up with calls from horny punters because the number was very close to that of a popular phone sex hotline – in German, '6' translates to 'sechs'.

During the twentieth century we went from that misty era when players and fans rode together to games on public transport to a time when Lambo-driving players are flogging and shilling anything that isn't nailed down, and clubs are being floated on the stock market. Goodbye poodles and budgies, hello million-dollar pay cheques. The original ideals of footie – 'a sport with collective democratic values, forever the people's game' is how David Conn

'No football club owner in his right mind would willingly invite an average agent into his academy, any more than a brothel owner would let a syphilitic nutter into his brothel.'

Crystal Palace chairman, Simon Jordan, in 2005

Cristiano Ronaldo meeting his contractual obligations in the duty-free area at Barajas International Airport, 2013.

describes them in his brilliant Man City exposé *Richer Than God* – have taken a backseat. Propelled by TV deals, the birth of the Premier League, celebrity culture, a new breed of agents, and then brand managers, and then social media, today's footie landscape is a Sodom and Gomorrah of financial opportunism.

Speaking of Sodom and Gomorrah … a mate of mine recently wandered into a promotional event at the Cannes Film Festival. My pal found himself standing in the shadow of several giant ice-sculptures of Cristiano Ronaldo, in signature pose. Multiple fragrance bottles had been cunningly frozen into Ronaldo's head, limbs and torso. But all was not well. Reality bites, and melts, and the sculptures were turning to water faster than Ronny Heberson's 2006 penalty kick (131 mph). The bottles were poking through the rapidly thinning face, legs, torso and arms of frozen Ronaldo in a terrifying way. Hordes of attendees began Instagramming and tweeting the unfolding spectacle.

A brief word about social media: footie players, being largely millennials, are enthusiastic users of Twitter, Instagram and Facebook. Supervision, however, is critical. In 2016 Sunderland striker Victor Anichebe diligently tweeted the following: 'Can you tweet something like: Unbelievable support yesterday and great effort by the lads! Hard result to take! But we go again!' Including the PR director's instructions in front of your tweet definitely gets a social media red card.

Footballers become fashion designers

When I hear that a footie player has decided to dive headlong into the fashion business, every orifice slams shut. Call me pessimistic, but I immediately have visions of the bloke in question blowing through his capital – in his excitement to book all the hottest models for his show, the lad in question forgets to invite any store buyers – and ending up living with his mum, without enough cash to become a poodle-fancier, never mind open a wool shop.

In 2016, David Beckham began a collaboration with the venerable British house of Kent & Curwen, a project billed: 'Reimagined British classics in partnership with David Beckham form a curated wardrobe for the modern man'. The retired Beckham only gets smarter. By simply partnering with an established company – he is co-owner and muse – he avoids the cost and the operational headaches associated with a start-up. Will it be a success? Not many blokes want to dress like Psychedelic Ninjas, but there is no shortage of those who want to dress like now-classic-former-sarong-wearing Beckham. David told Mr Porter: 'It's everything that I would be seen in, it's things that I have worn in the past, it's things that we have discussed me wearing in the future.' Beckham then reassuringly tells us that, 'This is not a scam'.

In today's footie world there are a number of brave individuals who are attempting to launch their own fashion lines. Though footballers inevitably struggle to make their mark in this competitive field, they appear to have no problem coming up with a sassy brand name. Alex Song has a clothing line he has dubbed 'Systeme Tchakap', which, according to the *Daily Mail*, 'refers to an African way of life, living with a certain freedom and independence'. On a slightly less spiritual note, in 2016 Leicester City's Christian Fuchs launched a fashion line of T-shirts and sweatshirts. The name? NoFuchsGiven.

Brooklyn and Becks wearing dad's heritage-con-twist Kent & Curwen fashion line, in 2017.

MR LENOIR

THE NEW ERA OF DJIBRIL CISSE

Djibril Cissé's collection is named 'Monsieur Lenoir', which sounds so cheesy that it's cool.

Right before his 2016 move from Paris Saint-Germain to Manchester United, Zlatan Ibrahimović launched A-Z, a line of not-half-bad sportswear. 'It's time to take over', declared Ibrahimović, after a presentation that featured strobe lights and modern dancers. With his signature humility – and sounding just a tad Trumpian – he reassured the press: 'This is the people's brand and I'm the people's man. That's the way it is. We will take over, trust me. We are going up against the big companies.' Any remaining scepticism about his ability to accomplish global domination was vanquished when, in August 2017, Zlatan launched a superhero mobile game called 'Zlatan Legends'.

Is Zlatan headed for a full-time career in the clothing business?: 'My future is A-Z. Follow A-Z and you will see my future.'

TOO SEXY FOR MY SHIRT

WHEN FOOTBALLERS BECOME FASHION MODELS

In 2017 LA Galaxy players Sebastian Lletget, Ariel Lassiter, Brian Rowe, A.J. DeLaGarza, Jelle Van Damme and Gyasi Zardes scored leading roles in the ad campaign for heritage suit-maker Samuelsohn, the official sponsor of the LA Galaxy. The leaping, high-kicking Galaxy lads dutifully emphasized the stretch properties of Samuelsohn's high-performance suit fabrics. 'Gyasi went as far as to split his pants', recalls Brighton-born art director and former casual Andrew Wren, who oversaw the shoot.

S P O R T
The Kooples

Eric & Rachida have been a couple for 10 years

Who is the hairy unsmiling bear with knitted hat and the piercing gaze? Ooh-aah! It's Canton-a! The greatest footie philosopher/model of all time.

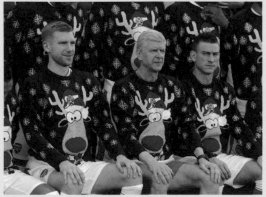

Clubs take a sadistic delight in forcing managers and players to model all manner of yuletide finery.

The lost art of hat modelling: Graham Moore (Chelsea), Bobby Moore (West Ham) and Eddie Firmani (Charlton Athletic) giving us 'Blue Steel' c. 1963.

'I must admit I have a dressing room curiosity over Beckham. I want to see if he's as equipped as he is in the underwear adverts', revealed AC Milan striker Marco Borriello in 2008, during Beckham's loan spell in Italy.

Undie world

There is something new on every footballer's career bucket list, something you won't find in the trophy cabinet: scoring that underwear deal! Sprawling in your skivvies, bathing in female/ gay objectification, Zoolandering into the lens of a camera while praying your package still looks acceptably prominent has become a great way to cap off a career.

In the 1980s, underwear was photographed on hot-bod models like Jeff Aquilon and Tony Ward. In the '90s ripped celebs like Antonio Sabato Jr. and Marky Mark picked up the slack. Footie players of the Eighties and Nineties were ok for aftershave and crisps, but not considered hip or pretty enough for homoerotic Bruce Weber underwear shoots. This was also the period of the dissolute footie player, like Paul Merson or Mick Quinn. Would they even show up for the shoot? Would they have beer bellies and love handles?

In fairness to all concerned, footie players are very polarizing figures. Throw a Man Utd player into a pair of branded Y-fronts and all the Liverpool fans will incinerate the contents of their underwear drawers and instigate a full-scale boycott. Sometimes it takes a foreigner like Calvin Klein, a guy unphased by team rivalries, to take the plunge. In 2003 Calvin Klein risked alienating many Spurs supporters when he shot Arsenal winger Freddie Ljungberg, oiled up and smouldering, in his new line of Pro-Stretch undies. Freddie was an obvious choice. The handsome Swede already had two League titles and two FA Cups under his gusset (a third lay in his future). At the time he was noteworthy for his shaved head and his ink, a look that was soon to become ubiquitous to the point of insanity, quite possibly courtesy of this landmark advertising campaign.

In 2012 Becks collaborated with H+M on a line of bodywear. Ferocious promotion included a Guy Ritchie-directed commercial, which featured a half-naked Becks zipping through backyards and swimming pools à la Burt Lancaster in the 1968 movie *The Swimmer*. In 2014 Real Madrid's James Rodríguez flaunted his bits in a collaboration undie collection for Colombian panty-maker Bronzini. Two years later he was twanging the elasticated waistband on Calvin Klein's briefs and square-cuts. Like his teammate Ronaldo, James's calling card is his extreme prettiness and his smooth bod. The ladies dig it, and when it comes to selling men's undies, women are the primary target. Current stats reveal that women are responsible for 50 per cent of underwear purchases,

In 2013 Cristiano Ronaldo launched his CR7 range of bulge-enhancing foundation garments. The bold, package-thrusting ads confirmed Cristiano's position as the undie-porn king of the world.

and, more importantly, they are largely responsible for the initial brand selection. They also skew the stats by purchasing men's undies online using the hubby's credit card. Either way, it's all about appealing to the girls, hence the oiled and shaved porno-bods. It's all a far cry from the nineteenth century and the lads of Newton Heath, with their rock-hard balls and their mud-caked clogs.

The shaving and oiling and commercialization of football is an inexorable, inevitable force that has changed the landscape forever and depresses the crap out of many die-hard fans. I would reassure these worthy individuals that it would be impossible to erase the original democratic ethos of footie: it is too entrenched. There is cause for optimism: the global shill that continues to engulf the beautiful game has, paradoxically, underscored the need to maintain that old-school meat-pie *authenticity*. Authenticity has become a fixation and a relentless buzzword. I have yet to listen to a podcast or read an article where the A word is not mentioned. Football has always and will always celebrate its heritage with landmark stats and beautiful memories. Despite all the logos and bungs – and maybe because of them too – the muddy history and super-butch authenticity of the game is memorialized and discussed with increasing fervour and appreciation.

WATCH OUT!

Cantona's collaborations with the Swiss avant-garde company Hautlence are enhanced by his signature philosophizing: 'the watch is about prison and freedom, death and life.' All this can be yours for a mere £17K.

'ROLEX WATCHES, GARAGES FULL OF FLASHY CARS AND MANSIONS, SET UP FOR LIFE, FORGOT ABOUT THE GAME, LOST THE HUNGER THAT GOT YOU THE WATCHES, CARS AND MANSIONS.'

Manchester United captain Roy Keane, after the 2002 Champions League semi-final defeat

In 2016 Andy Carroll was driving home from West Ham's Rush Green training ground in his £100,000 Mercedes G-Wagon when two masked motorcyclists blocked his path, pulled out a gun and demanded his watch. Andy called the cops and then floored it back to training, successfully eluding the highwaymen. Four days later Bournemouth attacking midfielder Jordon Ibe was relieved of his Rolex at knifepoint. And just before Christmas, masked men broke into the Victorian mansion of Liverpool's Roberto Firmino, making off with £70,000 in 'jewellery, watches and clothing', which could well mean they stole a single watch. In October 2017, 6ft 5in England goalie Joe Hart was gassing up his car in Essex when a moped gang zoomed in and relieved him of his phone, wallet, and yes, his watch. Are we looking at a possible trend here?

For some girls the answer to the financial challenges of life is to marry a footballer. Since men do not stand much chance of finding a footballer husband (one day?), they are better served to hunt them down and steal their watches. How can robbers possibly suss out which particular footballers are wearing expensive watches? Easy – they all are.

The 2016 Euros was a great time for casing the footie watch collections: Ronaldo wore a £4,000 Tag Heuer, tweeting, 'Time to relax and bring out my Tag Heuer Carrera to fuel me up before the big match!'; Jack Wilshere flaunted an Audemars Piguet Royal Oak Offshore priced at £26,900. Daniel Sturridge coughed up £70,000 for the Perpetual Calendar version. Meanwhile Jamie Vardy did himself proud with a £27,380 rose-gold Hublot.

'PEOPLE SAY I'M COCKY BECAUSE I HAVE TWO CARS AND A DIAMOND WATCH. BUT THAT MEANS THAT NINETY PER CENT OF FOOTBALLERS ARE COCKY.'

Newcastle and England midfielder Kieron Dyer, 2004

Rolex watches were also ubiquitous at the Euros: Ryan Bertrand wore a £6,100 Rolex Datejust; Eric Dier showed restraint with a £4,300 Rolex Explorer; Danny Rose soared with a £32,680 Rolex Skydweller, and landlocked Kyle Walker sailed away with a £12,600 Yachtmaster. Conclusion: in an era when the entire world relies on smartphones for accurate timekeeping, footie players continue dropping stupendous – some might say stupid – amounts of cash on prestige timepieces.

George Best makes a new friend.

> 'I prefer to win titles with the team ahead of individual awards or scoring more goals than anyone else. I'm more worried about being a good person than being the best football player in the world.'
>
> Lionel Messi

10. Nabbing the Silverware

What to Wear?

In 1968 George Best won the Manchester United Player of the Year award. That same year he also snagged the European Cup, the FWA Footballer of the Year award (as pictured), the Football League First Division Top Scorer and the Ballon d'Or, an international gong with massive prestige.

His acceptance outfit for the Footballer of the Year award is smart but stunningly understated: a white shirt, a shiny narrow tie and a tweedy sportsjacket. Dressing up in fancy frills and tuxedos was not the priority back then, even for spiffy George. Awards ceremonies were more about the bevvies.

In his memoir *Who Ate All the Pies?*, Portsmouth legend Mick Quinn recalls the joys of winning the Player's FA award. Off he trots to a fancy Park Lane hotel, where he proceeds to get 'absolutely bladdered on lager and champagne'. Footballers not only took pride in getting bladdered on free booze at awards shows, they also took pride in describing the experience in a seemingly infinite number of ways: trolleyed, trousered, legless, arseholed, ratted and rat-arsed being just the tip of the iceberg.

All this ratting and arse-ing produced a noteworthy side effect: legendarily incoherent acceptance speeches. The combo of free booze plus lectern has consistently created problems for footballers. When Portsmouth reached the First Division under Alan Ball in 1987, the entire team, already quite bladdered, was invited to a mayoral reception where the champers flowed and they each got a chance to address a crowd of 7000 Pompey fans. 'I've got a little appeal', declared midfielder Vince Hilaire, enigmatically, adding, 'If anyone sees a pair of sunglasses lying around, they're mine.'

1973: Gerd Müller (left) gets the Silver Boot and Eusébio gets
the Gold. Note the massive lapels and the bagel-sized tie knots.

Clockwise from top left:

1995. The dignified and deserving George Weah, the only player to win the World, European and African Player of the Year awards.

Zinedine Zidane, the only person in history who looks better with no hair, clutching his Ballon d'Or in 1998.

Born in the Czech Republic, but his hair is straight outta Malibu. Pavel Nedvěd gave us award-winning surfer-dude locks, on the occasion of his 2003 Ballon d'Or win.

Fabio Cannavaro, serving sombre, dapper Neapolitan style, while smooching his Ballon d'Or in 2006.

Half a century after George Best's FWA award, no footballer is wearing tweed, getting legless or making bladdered speeches to collect the silverware. Smartphones have made such displays thoroughly inadvisable. The risk of being uploaded before you have even sobered up has proven to be a successful deterrent. For good or for bad, the emphasis has shifted from boozing to dressing up: *How do I look? Let's take a selfie!*

Messi goes to Hollywood: a saga of award-winning fashion

The red carpet, that relentless fusion of fashion and celebrity that unfurls every time Hollywood decides to auto-fellate, has now infected the world of football. With its endless trophy moments and awards presentations, footie was doomed to succumb, and succumb it did. A watershed moment came in 2010 when the Ballon d'Or and the FIFA Player of the Year award merged, and suddenly the world of footie had its very own Academy Awards. In the intervening years, Messi and Ronaldo have tried to out-fashion each other at this event. Ronaldo has won the award three times, and Messi five. As I will painstakingly detail here in a forensic year-by-year examination, he has also out-vamped Ronaldo in the fashion stakes.

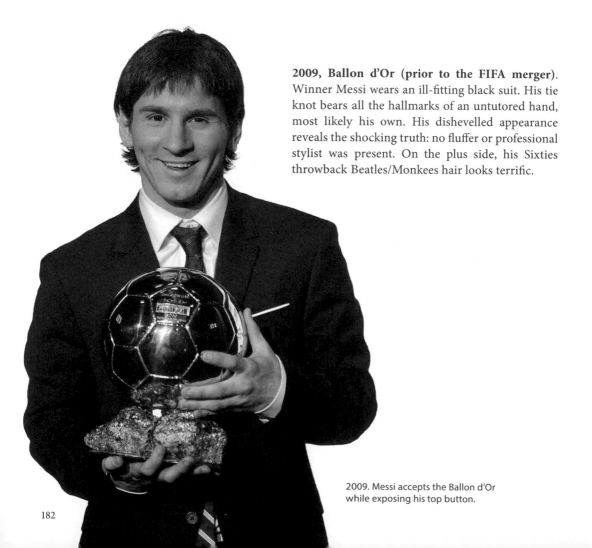

2009, Ballon d'Or (prior to the FIFA merger). Winner Messi wears an ill-fitting black suit. His tie knot bears all the hallmarks of an untutored hand, most likely his own. His dishevelled appearance reveals the shocking truth: no fluffer or professional stylist was present. On the plus side, his Sixties throwback Beatles/Monkees hair looks terrific.

2009. Messi accepts the Ballon d'Or while exposing his top button.

2010, FIFA Ballon d'Or. The year of the big merger – a watershed moment. Dolce & Gabbana to the rescue! This year Messi upgrades to a tux, and what a tux! Silk panné velvet with silk-satin lapels and matching bow tie. The Seventies porn-star hair adds a touch of dégagé, which prevents Messi looking too self-important. Every aspect of his appearance has been carefully considered. Celebrity styling has arrived.

2010. Messi, looking suave, soigné, and very *Ocean's Eleven*, wins again.

Messi, thickly upholstered in deep amethyst velvet, collects his third Ballon d'Or in 2011.

2011, FIFA Ballon d'Or. How to switch things up, without simply Xeroxing the black tux? Let's try a dab of colour. Stefano Gabbana & Domenico Dolce unearth a bolt of gorgeous purple velvet, enough for a jacket and waistcoat. The resulting outfit is hip and glamorous, with a whiff of Austin Powers. Speaking of whiffs, one can only imagine, with two layers of thick luxury velvet girding his torso, how Messi must have schvitzed on the evening in question. Hopefully his stylist had the presence of mind to provide 'pit-pads'.

Schvitzing notwithstanding, the outfit is a success. The satin edging, the sharp fit, fresh haircut and the narrow tie accomplish something important: Messi looks different from last year. Clearly Barça's #10 is just going to keep winning this particular award, and clearly he needs to look different every time he shows up, otherwise the history books will get very confused.

2012, FIFA Ballon d'Or. Purple (last year) is out, and a black tux (the year before last) is not going to cut it. Clearly busting a gut to continue upping the fashion stakes, Domenico Dolce & Stefano Gabbana do something rash, literally. They cover Messi in spots, including his bow tie. Looking for an explanation of some kind, the *Daily Mail* suggests this might be a homage to the spotty jacket worn by Maradona in 1995. The media smells blood. They seize upon the dots, and begin to speculate: are we seeing a pattern of fashion exhibitionism? What, pray, will he wear next year?

2012: spot the winner.

A blaze of glory? Or a disco inferno? Messi loses out to Cristiano Ronaldo in 2013.

2013, FIFA Ballon d'Or. Lionel Messi makes history. He bravely, and boldly, dares to go where no five foot seven inch-tall Argentinian has gone before. Two words: flaming shantung. In 2013, Signor Messi wears an extraordinary suit of lights made from shiny red shantung silk. It is a revelatory moment. The paradox of Messi – the unassuming lad with the groaning shelf of silverware – is nowhere more evident than in the photographs of this occasion. There he is, sitting mutely, shyly and inscrutably, encased in a raging, blazing forest fire of red bespoke Dolce & Gabbana.

When Messi fails to take home the Ballon d'Or, the inflammatory suit takes the fall. This garment explodes into a Mount Etna of tabloid lava. The populist rabble, with its conformist ideas about style, disdains Messi's fashion choices in no uncertain terms.

Memes abound, comments spew forth: is he off to the circus or the nut house? Like George Best in his sombrero and Gazza with the plastic breasts, Messi's red suit is instantly and forever after iconic, and mockable.

The world lost sight of the fact that what it should really have been expressing at that particular moment was not disdain, but gratitude. Award shows are boring and turgid occasions. Messi's fabulous red three-piece provided a memorable hot-poker-up-the-bum moment of unconventional bravado. While winner Ronaldo looks insanely elegant – in his scalpel-cut tux he reminds one of a Monaco croupier or a magnificent gigolo – it is Messi who keeps taking the fashion risks. For shits and giggles I popped into my local Dolce & Gabbana store and asked about the price of the custom Messi shantung suits: $10,000.

2014: Purple pain. Messi once again loses out to Ronaldo.

2014, FIFA Ballon d'Or. If red is not your lucky colour, let's try purple again, but this time Dolce & Gabbana add a little twinkle-weave. Second prize again. Style pointer: Messi's red-carpet outfits are theatrical and outrageous, but please take note of the simple, pared-down styling. If he wore them with chains and ruffles (as I might) he would look kitschy and old-fashioned (as I might). The minimal styling keeps Messi looking youthful and sharp.

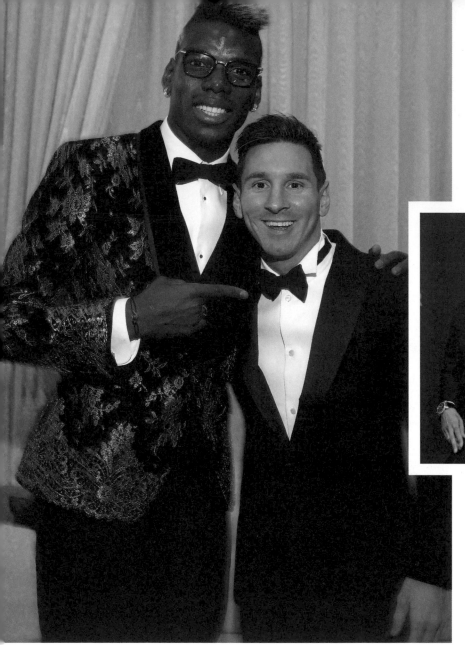

2015: winner Messi gives a nod to Downton Abbey, while Pogba adopts a daring, post-modern mash-up of nerd, punk and Vegas.

Allegedly, both Neymar and Messi were dressed by Giorgio Armani for the 2015 ceremony. Neymar scored a jaunty chapeau.

2015, FIFA Ballon d'Or. Third time lucky? Clearly a little concerned about becoming the Liberace of footie red carpets, a chastened Messi shows up in a restrained dressing-for-dinner tux with a wing collar. Unimpeachably elegant, but less memorable, he is also the winner. Footballers are such a super-stitious bunch, I become concerned that daring fashion choices will, in both Messi's mind and those of his competitors, be associated with losing, while classic tuxes will now signify wins.

Ronaldo puckers up for the FIFA Best Player award 2016.

2016. The Ballon d'Or and FIFA go their separate ways. Ronaldo wins the 2016 Ballon, but there is no dress-up ceremony. CR7 picks up the award in a boardroom, looking spiffy but unremarkable. All eyes are on the new FIFA Best Awards scheduled for 9 January 2017.

The nominees are Ronaldo, Messi and Antoine Griezmann of Atlético Madrid. Having won the 2016 Euros, the Champions League and the UEFA Super Cup, Ronaldo is favoured to win. But will he win on the red carpet? How will he out-tux Messi and the other attendees at a sparkling event co-hosted by Eva Longoria and Diego Maradona?

Psychedelic Ninja Dani Alves arrives in a rock and roll version of black tie, the lynchpin of which is a heavily embellished black leather zipped blouson and matching booties. Sergio Ramos kicks it old school with silk-satin and black velvet. And CR7?

His look might best be described as 'The Night Manager meets the Ralph Lauren Store Manager'. Instead of a tuxedo, winner Ronaldo opts for a vivid blue double-breasted custom suit, spread-collared business shirt and striped tie. His most noteworthy accessory is his new WAG, a Longoria-lookalike named Georgina Rodríguez.

And Messi? According to his club, he stayed in Spain 'to prepare for an upcoming Copa del Rey game against Athletic Bilbao'. I am guessing that for shy Messi these events are beyond excruciating, even when he wins, and even when the stylist remembers his pit-pads. On a night when he knows he is going home empty-handed? Torture.

2017. The FIFA Best Player Awards take place at the London Palladium, on a stage which has been graced by every flamboyant rocker, drag queen and sequined diva in the history of entertainment. Can the lads rise to the occasion? Will Messi and Ronaldo and the other top players continue to exceed our shantung expectations and caviar dreams?

Other than Alves (embellished black leather mariachi bolero) and Neymar (cranberry tux with matching tie), the awardees' fashion choices are staggeringly unremarkable. Ronaldo, the winner, and runner-up Messi are dressed alike in sharp-but-forgettable mod suits with narrow ties. They commit the ultimate fashion crime: they look *sensible*.

Messi's previous FIFA Ballon d'Or journey, aided and abetted by Dolce & Gabbana, provided the most clickbaity moments in football fashion history. Google 'Messi red suit' and you get 4.5 million hits. That red suit has become the Björk dead swan dress of the football world, a nostalgic moment of fashion daring. Just like Björk, Messi generously lobbed a bit of stylish provocation in our direction. Now I fear that the mockery of the internet has rendered Messi permanently gun-shy. His fearless red-suit years are behind him.

Will we see his like again? Of course we will. Even as I write there are embryonic Messis kicking balls in far-flung dusty corners of the world, day-dreaming of the bicycle kicks and Ferraris in their futures, and of the fabulously flashy rock-star suits they will don to accept their gongs.

Final Thoughts

In his 2003 autobiography, former Portsmouth centre-forward Mick Quinn observed that, 'footballers like to think they are boss drinkers, boss gamblers and boss shaggers'. He forgets to mention that we, the fans, like to think they are as well.

Yes, footballers are the locus of our fandom, but there's more: footballers also exist for our vicarious pleasure. We might not be winning trophies, growling through the streets in a Maserati GranCabrio or a Lamborghini Aventador, or executing bicycle kicks, or wearing Saint Laurent jeans, or zipping about on private planes snuggling under Hermès blankets with top-shelf tottie, or pouring artisanal tequila down our throats – but somebody sure as hell better be doing it. In their strange meteoric footballing lives we need to see all our hopes and fantasies distilled and writ large, exploding and imploding.

A century and a half in the making, the culture that has built up around football clubs is stylish, bracing, rich, majestic, sometimes tragic, often ribald, and frequently poignant. My only hope is that the magic and madness continues and that the players of tomorrow, and also the managers, will surrender to the exhibitionistic and outrageous impulses that, combined with the on-pitch magic, keep footie in the headlines. We need players like Raheem Sterling, who has a car for every day of the week and who just bought his mum a house with a jewel-encrusted sink. We need cockatiels and ink and Ferraris. Footie needs spectacular gifted athletes, but it also needs flamboyant, stylish bad boys.

Football needs authenticity, humility and dignity … plus a smattering of tattooed and mohawked exhibitionist geniuses like Roma's Radja Nainggolan.

In 2009 Pep Guardiola paid tribute to one of the greats in today's game: 'Andrés Iniesta doesn't dye his hair, doesn't wear earrings and hasn't got tattoos. That may make him unattractive to the media, but he's the best.' Iniesta, the five foot seven inch-tall Barcelona central midfielder, is an astonishing sportsman and a very appealing bloke. An honest mensch. If you were stuck in a lift or hit by a FedEx truck, wouldn't you want him on the scene to hold your hand? But imagine a world where every player was an Iniesta.

Getting tarted up, and showing off, and yanking your hair into a man bun, and beating your chest … these are good things. If all the lads were to become too understated and humble, the footie world would be a less dynamic place. Not every lad needs to become a Psychedelic Ninja, but somebody does.

Further Reading

There is no shortage of not-so-fun footie books out there. In the course of researching this book, I slogged through many a self-congratulatory autobiography. In a desperate attempt to help you avoid the same fate, I offer you – in no particular order – my list of thumbs-up reads.

Paul Merson, *How Not to Be a Professional Footballer*
HarperCollins, 2011

Paul Gascoigne & Hunter Davies, *Gazza: My Story*
Headline, 2004

Paul McGuigan & Paolo Hewitt, *The Greatest Footballer You Never Saw: The Robin Friday Story*
Mainstream Publishing, 1998

The Secret WAG, *I Am The Secret WAG*
Penguin, 2014

Frank Worthington, with Steve Wells & Nick Cooper, *One Hump or Two? The Frank Worthington Story*
ACL & Polar Publishing, 1994

Eamon Dunphy, *The Rocky Road*
Penguin, 2014

Pelé, *Pelé: The Autobiography*
Simon & Schuster UK, 2007 (new edn)

George Best, *Blessed: The Autobiography*
Ebury Press, 2002 (new edn)

Ross Raisin, *A Natural*
Jonathan Cape, 2017

Alex Ferguson, *Alex Ferguson: My Autobiography*
Hodder & Stoughton, 2013

Stan Bowles, with Ralph Allen & John Iona, *Stan the Man: The Autobiography*
Paper Plane Publishing, 1996

Ray Parlour, *The Romford Pelé: It's Only Ray Parlour's Autobiography*
Penguin, 2017

Barney Ronay, *The Manager: The Absurd Ascent of the Most Important Man in Football*
Sphere, 2010

Hunter Davies, *The Glory Game*
Mainstream Publishing, 2000 (new edn)

Maarten Bax, *Sex, Drugs and Soccer: Most Famous Bad Boys in the World of Soccer*
Aerial Media, 2015

Mick Quinn, with Oliver Harvey, *Who Ate All the Pies? The Life and Times of Mick Quinn*
Virgin Books, 2004

Duncan Hamilton, *Provided You Don't Kiss Me: 20 Years with Brian Clough*
HarperCollins, 2007

David Conn, *The Fall of the House of Fifa*
Yellow Jersey, 2017

David Conn, *Richer Than God: Manchester City, Modern Football and Growing Up*
Quercus, 2012

Julie Burchill, *Burchill on Beckham*
Yellow Jersey, 2001

Sid Lowe, *Fear and Loathing in La Liga: Barcelona vs Real Madrid*
Yellow Jersey, 2014

Simon Kuper & Stefan Szymanski, *Soccernomics*
Nation Books, 2009

David Winner, *Brilliant Orange: The Neurotic Genius of Dutch Football*
Bloomsbury, 2001

Tina Moore, *Bobby Moore: By the Person Who Knew Him Best*
HarperCollins, 2005

Franklin Foer, *How Soccer Explains the World: An Unlikely Theory of Globalization*
HarperPerennial, 2010 (repr. edn)

Zlatan Ibrahimović, with David Lagercrantz, *I Am Zlatan Ibrahimović*
Penguin, 2013

Roy Keane, with Roddy Doyle, *The Second Half*
Weidenfeld & Nicolson, 2014

Tony Adams, with Ian Ridley, *Addicted*
CollinsWillow, 1999 (new edn)

Nick Hornby, *Fever Pitch: A Fan's Life*
Gollancz, 1992

Index

Picture Credits

Page

2 Courtesy the author
4 Olivier Ebanga/Anadolu Agency/Getty Images
6 McManus/BPI/REX/Shutterstock
8 Courtesy the author
10 Peter Robinson/Empics/PA
12 Eamonn and James Clarke/PA Images
15 Tom Schirmacher / AUGUST
16 Steve Schofield/Contour by Getty Images
17 Eamonn and James Clarke/PA Images
18 **left** Jasper Juinen/Getty Images
18 **right** Pete Goddard / Splash News
19 **left** Manchester Evening News
19 **top right** Michael Murdock / Splash News
19 **bottom right** Eamonn and James Clarke/PA Images
20 **left** Gerald O'Rourke/Goff Photos LLP
21 epa european pressphoto agency b.v./Alamy Stock Photo
22 **left** Andreas Rentz/Getty Images For IMG
23 **left** www.xposurephotos.com
23 **right** www.xposurephotos.com
24 Antonella Foglia / Splash News
25 Ross Robinson / WENN.com
26 Venturelli/Wire Image/Getty
27 Mike Poloway/UNP
28 Derek Preston/Paul Popper/Popperfoto/Getty Images
30 **top** Trinity Mirror / Mirrorpix / Alamy Stock Photo
30 **bottom** Patrice Fury/REX/Shutterstock
31 Popperfoto/Getty Images
32 ANL/REX/Shutterstock
33 Mirrorpix
34 **top** Trinity Mirror / Mirrorpix / Alamy Stock Photo
34 **bottom** Mirrorpix
35 Schirner/ullstein bild via Getty Images
36 Bentley Archive/Popperfoto/Getty Images
37 **left** Bob Thomas/Getty Images
37 **right** Bob Thomas/Getty Images
38 L'Equipe/Offside
39 **top** A. Jones/Express/Getty Images
39 **bottom** Mirrorpix
40 **top** Bob Thomas/Getty Images
40 **bottom** Mirrorpix
41 Mirrorpix
42 Mirrorpix
43 **top** Bob Thomas/Getty Images
43 **bottom** David Cannon/Allsport/Getty Images
44 **top** Dave Kendall/PA Images
44 **bottom** Bob Thomas/Getty Images
45 **left** Chris Bacon/PA Images
45 **right** REX/Shutterstock

46 **top** Martyn Goodacre/Getty Images
46 **bottom left** Tom Wargacki/Wireimage/Getty Images
46 **bottom right** Dylan Martinez/Reuters
47 OnEdition/REX/Shutterstock
48 **left** News Group Newspaper / News Syndication
48 **right** STEVE WOOD/REX/Shutterstock
49 **right** Kevin Mazur/Wireimage/Getty Images
50 Duncan Raban/PA Images
52 Catherine Ivill - AMA/Getty Images
53 **top** Stu Forster/Getty Images
53 **bottom** Jo Gidden / PA Images
54 REX/Shutterstock
55 **left** Mirrorpix
55 **right** Stuart MacFarlane/Arsenal FC via Getty Images
56 Colorsport
57 **top** Lutz Bongarts/Bongarts/Getty Images
57 **bottom left** Bob Thomas/Getty Images
57 **bottom right** Colorsport/REX/Shutterstock
58 Mirrorpix
59 **top** REUTERS / Alamy Stock Photo
59 **bottom** Malte Christians/Bongarts/Getty Images
60 **left** WENN Ltd / Alamy Stock Photo
60 **right** Visionhaus/Corbis via Getty Images
61 **top** VI Images via Getty Images
61 **bottom** Tony O'Brien/Action Images/Mirrorpix
62 AMA/Corbis via Getty Images
63 Valerio Pennicino/Getty Images
64 IBL/REX/Shutterstock
65 RANCK FIFE/AFP/Getty Images
66 JOHN THYS/AFP/Getty Images
69 **left** Eddie Keogh/Reuters/Mirrorpix
69 **right** Catherine Ivill/AMA/Corbis via Getty Images
70 AMA/Corbis via Getty Images
71 Imaginechina/REX/Shutterstock
72 **top** VI Images via Getty Images
72 **bottom** Jean Catuffe/Getty Images
73 Lars Ronbog / FrontZoneSport via Getty Images
74 Matthias Hangst/Getty Images
75 PATRIK STOLLARZ/AFP/Getty Images
76 **top** KENZO TRIBOUILLARD/AFP/Getty Images
76 **bottom** MCCFL / Splash News
77 Lars Ronbog / FrontZoneSport via Getty Images
78 BEN STANSALL/AFP/Getty Images
79 AMA/Corbis via Getty Images
80 **top right** Press Association Images
81 © Trevor Leighton
82 Action Press/REX/Shutterstock
83 Gebert/Epa/REX/Shutterstock
86 **top** Eamonn and James Clarke/PA Images
86 **bottom** Eamonn and James Clarke/PA Images
87 **top** Eamonn and James Clarke/PA Images
87 **centre** CM / Splash News
87 **bottom** Eamonn and James Clarke/PA Images
88 **top** Deano / Splash News
88 **bottom left** Chris Neill/Mirrorpix

Author's acknowledgements

Negi Darsses
Mark David
Michael Davies and Roger Bennett (Men in Blazers)
Will Frears
Joe Gaffney
Nathan Gale
Gerrard Gethings
Alice Graham
William Hibbert
Tim Higgins and Gill Griffiths
Allan Kennedy
Felicity Maunder
Andy McNicol
Camilla Morton
Jim Nutley
Nicolas Pauly
David L. Portilla
Sir Paul Smith
Simon Trewin
Heather Vickers
Simon Walsh
Andrew Wren

LAURENCE KING

Published in 2018 by
Laurence King Publishing Ltd
361–373 City Road
London EC1V 1LR
United Kingdom
Tel: +44 20 7841 6900
Fax: +44 20 7841 6910
e-mail: enquiries@laurenceking.com
www.laurenceking.com

© text 2018 Simon Doonan
This book was produced by
Laurence King Publishing Ltd, London

Simon Doonan has asserted his right under the
Copyright, Designs, and Patents Act 1988, to be
identified as the Author of this Work.

A catalogue record for this book is available
from the British Library.

ISBN: 978-1-78627-259-1

Design: Nicolas Pauly
Cover design and features: Intercity
Picture research: Heather Vickers
Senior Editor: Felicity Maunder

Printed in Slovenia

Front cover: photograph by Gerrard Gethings
Back cover: Cristiano Ronaldo and
Lionel Messi at the 2014 FIFA Ballon d'Or.
Action Press/REX/Shutterstock